DRINK TO THE BIRD

BENEDICT KIELY

Drink
to the
Bird

A Memoir

Methuen

For Frances

First published in Great Britain 1991
by Methuen London
Michelin House, 81 Fulham Road, London SW3 6RB

Reprinted in 1991

Copyright © 1991 Benedict Kiely

The author has asserted his moral rights
A CIP catalogue record for this book
is available from the British Library
ISBN 0 413 64990 3

Typeset by Deltatype Ltd, Ellesmere Port
Printed in England by Clays Ltd, St Ives plc

CONTENTS

'Well, Mr Flood, we have the harvest moon
Again, and we may not have many more;
The bird is on the wing, the poet says,
And you and I have said it here before.
Drink to the bird . . .'

From *Mr Flood's Party*
by Edwin Arlington Robinson

The Fingerpost Says . . .

These few words, as Savonarola must at some time or other have said, by way of direction and introduction.

It has taken me the length of this book and the most of one hundred thousand words to say au revoir to Omagh Town in the County Tyrone, and to the verdant land around that Town and to the people, therein and thereon, living and dead, that I knew.

Close to Omagh I was born, and in its streets and on the roads around it I grew up. Or was reared. We also had a house.

In the pages that follow I try to recall the place and the people as they were at that time. If I have not told all, in the current fashion, I may at least have told something about my Aunts, Kate and Rose and Brigid, and about some other decent people. It could also be that I have lingered overlong with some folk who made little mark on what used to be called the world's stage or on what we might now know as the gossip-columns or the chat-shows. But they did make some impression on me as we passed in the day, or in the night, and spoke to each other in passing.

The meticulous reader may detect digressions.

But the mind, such as it is, may surely, in this business of remembering, be allowed to meander. Even to take off for a while to fly, say, to Atlanta, Georgia, or the Blue Ridge mountains, or the hoarse Trinacrian shore of Oregon. Francis Drake, who was no Ariel, got as far as that in a little wooden boat.

It could also be that that same meticulous reader will herein find

Drink to the Bird

repetitions. But may not a septuagenarian with eight grandchildren, two in Ireland, two in England, four in Canada, may he not when he sits in the corner between the fire and the wall, where the poet, Austin Clarke, following tradition, placed the storyteller, may he not, I repeat, be occasionally permitted to repeat himself? And if you are writing a book of memories, it has to be, of necessity, about the things you remember not about matters that the reader, however percipient and considerate, thinks you should remember. And the grown, or aging, or aged man, remembering earlier days has also to be present all the time. And if, now and then, his mind, such as it may be, leaps back and forward, then that's only to be expected. He is fated to be in several places at the same time.

In the text that follows there are brief and, perhaps, puzzling references to a sojourn, also brief, that I spent in a Jesuit novitiate in the Irish midlands and to a sojourn, a little longer, in an orthopaedic hospital to the north of Dublin City. Let me try to explain.

Some time about the end of 1936, or the beginning of 1937, the Lord, or Somebody, suggested to me that I might enlist among the sons, or followers, of St Ignatius of Loyola. Actually I have the uneasy feeling that the suggestion came from Thomas Carlyle. And this is why I feel so.

If, at that time, you wished to put yourself forward to obey the call of God and become a Jesuit, the procedure, in Ireland, was that you went up to Upper Gardiner Street, in Dublin City, the road winding uphill all the way, and faced up to an interview, in the famous Ignatian house there, with three wise and experienced fathers of the Society. So off to Dublin I went in the company of, and under the guidance of, my mother who was naturally and/or supernaturally delighted that her baby boy was following the way to the stars.

What I remember most about that long-ago visit to Dublin was that Cyril Cusack was in the Abbey playing Bluntschli in *Arms and the Man*, and, as you may well imagine it, playing the part in high style, and there was me on the road to Manresa and listening to Bernard Shaw. My vocation may already have been in peril.

But about that interview!

Up the slope we went from the satanic pit of the Abbey Theatre to the celestial air of Upper Gardiner Street where the devil, or some of his crew, had once, physically if invisibly, tried to prevent Mathew Talbot, the saintly Dublin-working-man, from entering to worship. Nobody, seen or unseen, barred the door to me and, leaving my mother at her meditations in the church, I entered the residence and faced up to the three wise Fathers.

One was a Father Kieran, the Father Provincial of the Jesuits in Holy Ireland. He was small, plump and benevolent. Then there was a Father John Coyne, a tall, austere man whom I have often encountered over the years until quite recently and who has always spoken to me with courtesy and, I hope, forgiveness. And a Father Charles Doyle, a silverhaired, laughing man, brother in the Lord and, also, in the flesh, to that famous Father Willy Doyle who, as a war-chaplain, was killed at the Western Front and who had acquired the reputation, quite rightly for all me or the like of me would know, of being a saint of God. He may some day be, as the good people put it, raised to the altars.

So there were the three fine Fathers and there was me, and my mother praying in the church, and the sinful world outside on the streets of Dublin, going about its sinful business and not giving a fiddler's fi'penny fart for the threat I posed to its evil ways: and someone of the three Fathers asked me why I wished to become a Jesuit.

Now the brutal truth was that I did not know. But under the circumstances, and seeing that I had travelled all that far, I had to think of something. So I called to my aid my good friend, Thomas Carlyle, and came out with something that Carlyle had, with all the suavity and courtesy of Ecclefechan, Scotland, said about the Jesuits. What it was, or right or wrong, I cannot now remember. Something absolutely bloody, I might guess, out of the grindings and groanings of the 'Latter-Day Pamphlets'. But, as I may later on mention, I had at an early age a freak gift, nothing to do with intelligence, for remembering and rattling-off anything in prose or verse (but not in statistics) that I had read once or twice. And, like the whitefaced Fauntleroy that I was, I capped my quotation by saying that it was what poor Carlyle, who I am sure meant no harm, and other enemies of the Church (guess which) had said that determined me to join the Jesuits.

Why those good Fathers did not ordain me on the spot I still cannot understand. Somebody, perhaps, was praying for them and they had friends in the highest places.

Yet they accepted me as a novice.

That night I was brought to look at and to listen to, for the second time, Cyril Cusack reciting Bernard Shaw.

Facilis descensus Averno! How easy is the descent into Hell!

It was then, for the first time, apart from trips to and holidays in Dublin City, and Donegal and Sligo, that I took off from Omagh Town and the land around it in West Tyrone. To spend a dreaming year in the lush and green Irish midlands, going through the daily ritual of Jesuit life, as it was then meticulously arranged for neophytes, never quite certain what I was doing there or how I came to be there. A lot like life in general for a lot of us. But that is not to say that I was unhappy or discontented in the woods of Emo in the County Laois. Anything but. At any stage in a man's life dreams may be more reasonable than reality. Not to mention happiness. What, and the best authorities tell us so, what we have to worry about is when dreams create unhappiness.

A student in the faraway Wild West (in Berkeley, California) once asked Thomas Flanagan – professor, scholar and historical novelist – what was the greatest contribution the Irish had ever made to literature written in English. That learned man, who is somewhat given to quirky remarks which his friends describe as Flanaganisms, said: 'To burn Edmund Spenser out of Kilcolman Castle, during the Desmond Wars, and stop him writing about the Faerie Queene.'

Needless to say, Flanagan did not mean it, and being perhaps one of the few who have ever read, with attention, the entire works of Spenser, he hastened to explain his quasi-humorous remark to a somewhat humourless and indiscreet student: but thereafter was engaged for several years in soothing the wounded feelings of the chief Spenserian in that particular college.

Now we all owe a lot to Edmund Spenser and if your god is as Edmund Blunden said . . .

> Some love the mountains, some the sea,
> But a river god is the god for me.

And if your god is a river-god then you must bow your head to that great Elizabethan every time you cross a bridge. And he was particularly good on Irish rivers even if he did seem to think that they were all tributaries of the sweet and softly-flowing Thames.

As for myself I owe him a lot, including the title of a book. For when, fifteen or sixteen years after I had been there, I tried to write into a novel something of what I remembered of that novitiate, or House of Holinesse, I stole a title and an epigraph from Edmund Spenser:

> There was an Auncient House not far away,
> Renownd throughout the world for sacred lore
> And pure unspotted life . . .

The title of the novel was *There Was An Ancient House*. What else? At least I brought the spelling up-to-date. Then I rambled on, while the young fellow in question tries to work out where he is and what he is doing there. He is waking up in bed in the morning in a large room containing six beds, each bed cubicled off by white curtains. This large room is described as a Camarata. There are several Cameratae in the Ancient House. Camarata! What a lovely name for a beloved daughter or mistress, or something.

Anyway. Here was the poor boy, waking up:

> It was a white world. He opened his eyes slowly, wondering. He said
> to himself: How and When? Why? He repeated several times: Where?
> Pure white curtains on railings around his cubicle trembled in the
> flow of air from the open window. He touched the white coverlet
> with his right hand and thought that his hand was suddenly white,
> fragile. Sunlight came with the air through the window and
> brightened the white wall. Beyond the curtains somebody scraped a
> foot on the wooden floor, and coughed. Outside in the sunshine and
> free air a great-tit was squeaking, like an unoiled bicycle-pump. He
> thought again: Where? And, now that he was properly awake, he
> laughed at his own attempt to deceive himself, for he knew when and
> where and how but he wasn't too sure of why.
> So he shut his eyes and looked back and saw a town, a school, his
> first Communion morning, several girls, a clerestory window, angels
> carved in wood, a lifted golden monstrance, a visit to wise priests in a
> tall still house behind a church in the middle of a city.
> On his first Communion morning he had worn a jersey as white as
> the cubicle curtains and been chill with worry in case the host might
> touch his teeth. Afterwards, kneeling beside his mother he had prayed
> that he might be a priest. Dear Jesus, who hath this morning come
> into my soul for the first time, help me, when I grow up, to be a
> priest. Three Hail Marys that I may be able to be a priest. Then

home to porridge, rasher and eggs, tea, lemonade, money to spend
and down the sunny hometown to a photographer in a room above a
sweetie shop, and sixpence and a smile from the photographer, and
sweets in the shop on the way out from a smiling shopgirl who patted
him on the head, to his great pride and delight, because seeing her
dressed up and walking the way between her home and her shop he
had always thought her the stateliest lady in that town.

The town, too, was the centre of the world. It wasn't always sunny
as it had been on that morning. . .

So here I am home again in that ineluctable town.

Many thanks, Mr Joyce, for the loan of that lugubrious adjective.

But about that interlude in foreign parts. Or those two interludes.
One in the House of Holinesse. One in the House of Healing.

For, in sunshine or in shadow, the Town was always there, and real.
Every bit as real as the House of Holinesse in the deep, green Irish
midlands never quite was.

No world is rock real. As a certain poet in Dublin once said to me
when, as a young journalist, I was emerging one enchanted evening,
from a reception in a fashion-modelling agency, and had marvelled to
him about the unreality, or so it seemed to me to be, of the world in
which those beautiful creations pirouetted.

No world, the poet said sadly, is rock real.

But the woods of Laois were real, and the great oblong, stone
mansion in which, far from fashion models and, let us hope, any
Anthonian thoughts or diabolical-in-the-desert visions of them, the
novices moved and prayed and had their being, and all that. The
mansion was, indeed an ancient house: the work in the eighteenth
century of the great James Gandon who had given to Dublin the Four
Courts and the Custom House.

Edward VII of England, before Jehovah or Somebody anointed him
and made a King out of him, had slept a night or two in that great house
as the honoured guest, bestowing honour on the Earl of Portarlington
whose home the place was. It was, also, much to be hoped and prayed
for that no Jesuit novice ever wondered, by night or by day, as to which
Camarata Edward had slept in, or with whom. Alexandra, we may
chivalrously suppose.

To celebrate Edward's regal arrival the main avenue, a mile long and lined with graceful Wellingtonias, was laid with thick red carpet: and soldiers presented arms and bugles were blown. In a hospital ward in the Workhouse then, that is in 1937, still so-called, in the neighbouring town of Mountmellick, I spoke with an old soldier who, with the wind of a younger man, had sounded his trumpet on that heavenly occasion.

But by 1937 the red carpets were folded and stored away in more places than Emo Park in the County Laois, and greater foldings were to come: and gone, too, were the Earl and his saintly Countess Aline, something of a legend for a long time in that part of the country: and a new State forestry, organised by a new State, had grown almost as high as the Wellingtonias. The old, ornamental lake, the fringe of which had retained a few grey ghosts of classical statuary, was pike-infested to quite an alarming extent. Perhaps my one contribution to the life of the Society of Jesus may have been to set nightlines in that still and weedy water: the only poacher, a friend of mine was later to say, among the sons of St Ignatius. Well not, perhaps, the only one, but the others were after other fish and in other waters.

So there were we all, praying away and happy, most of us, in heavenly peace in the deep woods of Laois.

At weekly intervals we went out on long walks, very long walks which came under the heading of Recreation. As, indeed, they were. It was a fine and handsome and historic countryside to tramp through. For specified portions of our recreational time we spoke in the native Irish and even in the Latin Vulgate: the Path to Rome, as the man said. There was a specimen book of Latin conversation that began with the sentence: *Siste perumper, quaeso frater.*

Or, for the benefit of non-classicists: Stay a moment, Brother, I beseech you.

Inevitably, and unfortunately, the harmless little book became known as 'Sister Perumper', and that reverend Sister became a person, and an author, whose works could be humorously compared with the spiritual treatises of Mother St Paul who did, at the time, exist and did write. As also did Mother Mary Loyola. Whom I heard referred to by a fellow-novice, a soft-spoken man from Galway, as Mother Mary Lie Over. But since the man who deliberately made that play with the good lady's name is now a famous Jesuit and has carried the Cross as far away as Africa, I will not mention his name.

When we walked out into the countryside we wore any old clothes. Nothing clerical about us. So that the local people who, at that time, had not caught up with the Ignatian ideal, came to believe that in the Earl's oblong palace there was a school for the sons of gentlemen who had come down in the world. That was more than fifty years ago and in the Irish countryside some people still talked respectfully and regretfully of gentlemen.

The towns of the neighbourhood – Portarlington, Portlaoise, Mountmellick . . . etc. – were out of bounds for those walks, which was a pity. Lovely towns that, in later years, I was to have the joy of discovering.

And there was the most musically-named town of Monasterevan where, at that time, a notable man of music, John Count McCormack, lived in the great house of Moore Abbey on the banks of the river Barrow. Music, the poet said, built the towers of Troy. But my most vivid memory of musical Monasterevan is of standing in an icy east wind, on the towing-path under a canal-bridge, and chewing at two stuck-together slices of brown bread, our austere, walkabout, outdoor lunch, no liquid allowed unless the Lord, like Aaron, burst a spring on the side of the road. Later in life I had the privilege of meeting John McCormack and he told me that if I had then beaten on his door I would have been most welcome, and to better than brown bread. But there you are: the fine things in life you find out about too late.

There was the Huguenot town of Portarlington where the Duke of Wellington, and many another, had gone to school. There was the town of Portlaoise, then still commonly called Maryborough after a tragic queen: and the town of Mountmellick, a portion of which we were permitted to pass through when a party of three or four of us would walk, clerically-dressed as for a special occasion, and on a mission of mercy and comfort, we hoped, to visit the aged sick in the hospital wards of that aforementioned Workhouse.

But, also, there was, for splendour, Maryborough Heath, wide and windy acres echoing with hoofbeats, even if the Heath was by no means as spacious as the Curragh of Kildare: and beyond the Heath there was a range of low hills, a perfect backdrop for the castled Rock of Dunamase from which Rory O'More, the then Lord of Laois and more besides, had, in his days of glory, held out against Elizabethan invaders.

Resounding and inspiring ground to walk over. Yet even the

historical associations only seemed to emphasise the withdrawn unreality of the House of Holinesse, hidden in the trees. So where, on this pleasant earth, did I belong? To those green hills of Ulster and to that Town where I was born, settled for a long time among them? Where else was there?

But from any eminence, however slight, in that Laois countryside, you could look to the east and see the sun in the morning on the Dublin-Wicklow mountains, and then remember that Dublin City, and a lot of real people, were all over there at the foot of those mountains. Dublin was not yet, by no means, my town. But I had known it from an early age, and it had long been proved that Dublin did exist. From an early age I had known the place through my having had the good fortune to own an elder sister who was married to a genuine Dublinman, and living there. On that good sister, and on her genial husband, I had been allowed to inflict myself for the summer holidays, learning my way around the city on a simple, fool-proof plan.

That plan was to make my way, for a start, as far as Nelson's Pillar. The decent, disabled man still stood up there, watching his world (about to) collapse as the poet, Louis MacNeice, was to see him in the years of the Second World War. Nelson himself, or, rather, his graven or cast image, was to hold out until 1965 when some of the happy-go-lucky architects of the New Ireland, Éire Núa, and welt the floor, your trotters shake, blew him up or down, and hinted at their constructive plans for the lots of fun to come.

But in my days of exploration around the Pillar the electric trams creaked their joints and rubbed noses almost, and switched their tails and altered directions, as Leopold Bloom had observed them to do, and then took off, slowly but certainly, towards all points of the compass.

What I did was, quite simply, to take any old tram as far as the tracks and trolley that carried and motivated it went. Then, along that same route, I would walk back to the Pillar. Follow the tracks, Tom Stanley, the brother-in-law said, and you can't go wrong.

For reassurance, a numbered ship once in a while overtook me and sailed splendidly past and I would know I was, literally, on the right tracks. Stephen Dedalus who walked, or was made to walk, a lot of long distances around the town, might, or might not, have given his approval to my plan of discovery.

Threepence I kept in my pocket for the tramfare from the Pillar to my sister's house. Those three pennies were precious for there were days when, after walking back along a very long tramway route, I tottered as far as the Pillar, hot and thirsty and footsore. There was, though, one difficult day when, tempted by a complete John Milton, Latin poems and all, green-backed, and shabby as myself, and on a bookstall in Aungier Street in the South City, and selling for threepence . . .

It did not, at that moment, seem much to give away for the holus-bolus of Mr Milton, God-gifted organ-voice of England who, as we all know, shouldst be living at this hour: and I loved and treasured that book for a long time. But that day I had to sorefoot it all the way home from the pediment of Horatio Nelson. Englishmen all over the place. Yet I walked in style for I was a man on my own and not living according to any rule, holy or otherwise, except perhaps, and at that moment, by the regulations of the Dublin United Tramways.

Yes, stand on the Rock of Dunamase, or even on lesser heights in the rich land of Laois, and look to the east and there were the enchanted, rounded, blue mountains: and Dublin and life, at the roots of them.

Or waking at night in the Great House in which Royal Edward may have turned in his sleep, or something, one could hear the hooting of a train, sounding as lonely and faraway as the Colorado Trail. It was on the way, out there, *in mundo*, from Dublin or to Dublin. And even if Dublin was not for a few years to become my town it was still out there and alive, and many-headed, and waiting.

Then the serpent struck.

On a spot, previously unknown to me by name, but which I was to discover was known as the Third Lumbar. He, the serpent, or she for all I know, made himself, or herself, felt as if his, or her, fang, were a long, red-hot knitting-needle. He had, though, introduced himself to me before that moment. Back home in the Town of Omagh. When I was about sixteen. When I'd get out of bed in the morning, under maternal suasion, to trudge off, hail, rain or shine, to worship the Lord at eight o'clock Mass. Every sacred and sanguine morning. Down the six or seven concrete steps, down a steep slope, around a corner, along Kevlin Road and up Church Hill. But one fine morning the serpent struck for the first time: a demon, invisible as those presences that in Gardiner Street, in Dublin, endeavoured to keep that Christian stalwart,

Mathew Talbot, away from his devotions. Quite impossible for me that morning to go on walking, with spine erect, as the son of an old soldier should.

But if, always through life, I was low on strategy, I was a smart tactician and I had that move worked out. Halfways down Kevlin Road there was Hop McConnell's shop. Owned by a good Presbyterian family. Aged father with a limp and a stick. Hence, Hop. Lovely lady of a mother. Gentle son called Bob. And one great thing about the shop was that it had a windowsill about two feet from the ground. So that when the serpent stabbed and my back began to bend I could get my left foot on that windowsill, pretend to tie my shoe-lace, and hold on like hell until I was able to straighten up, and then walk on up Church Hill and over the place where the troopers of King James Stuart had once, on their way to the walls of Derry, rested their horses and themselves: as I may later mention. For I knew that my good father on his way to work would be hot on my heels, nor did I wish him to feel ashamed of a son who couldn't bloody well walk straight.

There can be no limit to the oddity of the secrets that young fellows, and young ladies, wish to keep to themselves.

Yet my father was by no means completely codded. Old soldiers have sharp eyes. Off and on he would say: 'Something wrong with your back.'

And I would swear like a trooper and protect the privacy of the serpent. Who, after a while, slithered off into some bosky shade and fell asleep. Lying dormant, was what the medical people, most aptly, called it. Serpents and bears and all sorts of people do that now and again. And my personal serpent came awake again and set-to with his hot fang in the garden and countryside around the House of Holinesse. Where there was a rule that all suspect matters relating to health should be reported to the Prefect of Health. By that time I was beginning to take life and rules, some of them, seriously. So I sold the pass on the serpent, as better and older people than myself once did, and forfeited the privilege of continuing to live in the garden.

Odd thing, though. A school friend of mine, Joseph Gilroy, who grew up to be a noted financier, kept saying over the years that he remembered exactly when I got that back-injury. There were a crowd of us, young fellows, playing street football in a sidestreet, Campsie Cresent, in Omagh Town. It was Gaelic football, which meant a lot of high kicking and jumping and catching. So I jumped and somebody knocked me behind the knees and I landed on my ass on the tarmacadam, and stood up painfully and said: Oh Jasus, me back.

Or other devotional words with that connotation.

It amuses me, or something, to think that if we had been playing soccer football and keeping ourselves and the ball on the carpet, as the phrase went, I might now be an elderly, saintly Jesuit asking young aspirants why, under God and before men, they ambitioned to become Jesuits.

And so on to the second interlude. In the House of Healing.

So, three times only in my life have I been, so far, in hospital and that is two times more than my father ever was, and he walked around a lot and almost made ninety. He went once, and briefly, when he was eighty-five, but rapidly decided that he could die more comfortably at home, where he could hear familiar voices talking all the time and his own clock chiming away the hours. It had a mellow musical chime.

The only other medical experiences he ever had involved a toothache, a sprained ankle and a hiccough. The sprain was rubbed and rapidly cured by an old man who had a gift that way, and who would accept payment only in twists of chewing-tobacco. The hiccough survived for two days of agony and comedy, and then went away of its own accord. But the curing of the toothache had something ferociously Gothic about it.

There was at that time and in our Town a sound doctor who also pulled teeth. The title of dentist was then little known, that of orthodontist had never been heard of. But that doctor also pulled corks. More corks than teeth. To help him to face the ordeal, my father, who hadn't had a drink for a long time, had a resiner (rozziner) of brandy, than marched bravely to face the forceps and to find that the doctor had been more diligently at the brandy than he, my father, had. And for no better reason than that he, the doctor, liked the stuff.

In the wrastling match that followed the doctor pulled the patient out of the chair and the two of them fell on the floor. But when the doctor stood up he waved the forceps and said that there it was. And there, indeed, the tooth was.

*

So that I hadn't much of a medical family-history to draw on when I found myself in hospital for the first time and, as it happened, for eighteen months. The memory of my arrival in that hospital came back to me quite vividly on a day, thirty-three years afterwards, when a blind man called Michael, whom I had never met before, spoke to me in a bus in Dublin City. He was a tall, greyheaded, handsome man. Since he was blind he recognised me only because he had heard my mournful, Scots-Irish voice on a certain radio programme. Because of something I had said on that programme he asked me: 'Would I be right in thinking that you knew the famous surgeon, the late Henry Macauley?'

'Knew him,' I said. 'Without him I would not be sitting here in this bus nor able to walk about when I got outside it.'

With sad amusement I remembered that spring day when I first met the great surgeon, one of two famous medical brothers. And the family name still continues in medicine in Dublin.

For the Prefect of Health in the House of Holinesse had passed me on to see the doctor in the town of Portlaoise, and the doctor had passed me on to Dublin for an X-ray, and the findings of the X-ray landed me flat on my back on a mattress with a fracture-board under it, and then onto a Whitman, no relation of Walt, spine-frame in Cappagh Orthopaedic Hospital on the outskirts of what was then the village of Finglas, on the northern outskirts of the city of Dublin.

There, for eighteen months, I had, from the wide open-air balcony, another fine view of the hills beyond and above Dublin. To contrast with the vision of those same hills from the faraway dreamland of Laois. Down somewhere at the root of those hills were the streets and the people of Dublin. William Morris, I did honestly remember, had written somewhere about the roots of the mountains.

But to me, as I lay there in my first week in Cappagh Hospital, and ready to carry, or be carried by, my cross: two parallel steel bars with canvas stretched tightly between them, on which subtle structure the patient lay flat and was spancelled down as to chest and knees and feet
. . .

Ready to carry my cross, I say, and positively dropsical with Christian virtue. And then there appeared the man who could give limbs to the halt. Sight to the blind nor hearing to the deaf were not within his bailiwick.

*

Henry Macauley in appearance was the perfect surgeon of romantic fiction. Immaculately dressed: I do remember that on that day he wore a dark grey suit with a sort of pinstripe. He had the right sort of wrinkles on his forehead and at the corners of his eyes. Crows' feet? Assuredly, he had crows' feet at the corners of his eyes. He and his brother Charles, too, were part of a patriotic legend. As medical students they had in the Civil War in 1922 gone, under shellfire, into the Four Courts to bring help to the wounded and what they could to the dying. Naturally I wanted to cut a good appearance before this man.

About the usages of the world of medicine I knew just enough to call a surgeon Mister and not Doctor. So after the formal handshake we had a few words on the spring weather, and on the view from the balcony, of Dunsink Observatory and the Dublin-Wicklow mountains. Then we had a few words about the Jesuits and about what they were up to those fine days and, after that, I grandly decided to put on my act. So I said: 'Mr Macauley, can you tell me how long exactly I'm going to be here?'

You see I had been thinking bravely and vaingloriously in terms of three months as the teetotal tolerable limit.

'You really want to know,' he said.

'Yes, Mr Macauley. I think it would be better.'

He looked at me for a while. He was smiling. And, I suppose, sizing me up. Then he said: "How about eighteen months. Give or take a day."

Just for a moment then I did not see the blue mountains nor Dunsink Observatory, nor Mr Macauley. If I had not been securely tucked and tied into my bed, my knees might have buckled. Then he laughed an easy sort of friendly laugh, and I found that I was laughing with him. He was right, too, to the day, about the eighteen months but, after that first meeting, I trusted him so much that I didn't give a damn.

At that encounter I think that I really lost my religious vocation, as it used to be, and may still be, called. Wildly assuming, that is, that I ever had one. Or, to put it all more exactly, faced with the laughter of that good and wise and generous man who was to remain my friend, I became more or less human and ceased, I hope, being the prig that so many young people are.

After the warm laughter of the great surgeon, the nuns and the nurses, God bless 'em, did the rest.

The Reverend Mother was the great Mother Polycarp who, among other achievements, had built the place: a woman of courage and humour and always with divine thanksgiving on her tongue. She was, also, and for laughs and curiosity, sister to Dr Cummins, eye-specialist and friend to Seán O'Casey.

Then one day another nun of the community, a Sister Francesca, came to my bedside to visit and console, or something, me. On her shoulder there was perched a green, raucous and quite vicious parrot called Andy. Who had already achieved a dubious fame by sneaking out from underneath a bed and wickedly biting a wardsmaid on the ankle.

Now Sister Francesca had discovered me, in my retreat, reading poetry of all things, and rightaway she began to tell me how the poet Pádraic Colum and her brother had jubilantly agreed on a title for Colum's collection: *Wild Earth*. From Colum's poem: 'Poor Scholar of the 1840s':

> And what to me is Gael or Gall?
> Less than the Latin or the Greek –
> I teach these by the dim rush light
> In smoky cabins night and week.
> But what avail my teaching slight?
> Years hence, in rustic speech, a phrase,
> As in wild earth a Grecian vase!

So Sister Francesca said to me: 'They talked about wild earth.' And I said: 'Turf mould. Or: the Bottom of the Irish Bog.'

Then she went on her way, laughing, and the green bird, quite obviously passed on to her by Long John Silver, screaming from her shoulder.

Too cute I was to show my ignorance by asking her who her brother was or had been. Until the hospital chaplain, Fr Joe Furlong, the curate priest from Finglas village, said to me: 'That old battleaxe, Francesca. A great and good woman, believe it or not. She does great work for the poor. You may not know it, Ben boy, but you are meeting great people. That brother she talks about was the poet Thomas MacDonagh who, as we all know, was murdered by the British in 1916 . . . Listen to her. She'll educate you.'

To Francesca I listened almost every day of my internment. And visited her regularly afterwards until she went off to Heaven where she is still talking with Andy, the green parrot, on her shoulder, making mockery of those eternal angels and, perhaps, of Jehovah himself. She may, like many another, have failed to educate me. But to be allowed to listen to her was a privilege and a joy.

Then came Fr Aubrey Gwynn, Jesuit and professor of medieval history in University College, Dublin, to, guess what, give a retreat to the nuns. He was one of a famous learned family, some of them Protestant, some Catholic, most Protestant, and so long and closely associated with Trinity College, Dublin (Queen Elizabeth's cesspool, Fr Furlong used to say, meaning the first Elizabeth) that it was a sort of a Dublin joke to rattle off: Trinity is Gwynnity and Gwynnity is Trinity.

Fr Aubrey came to see me every day of his stay and frequently, out of the kindness of his heart, afterwards. He talked about everything from his first meetings with Hilaire Belloc to the fun it was to read Wild West stories in French translations. Now that was great company for a young fellow with literary aspirations. And particularly since the younger Jesuits visited regularly, bearing books, a generosity that I have never forgotten. It takes a lot of books to keep you going for eighteen months.

Although Sister Finbarr, whose brother was Frank Gallagher, a noted old revolutionary and the first editor of Eamon de Valera's *The Irish Press*, thought, did Sister Finbarr, that too much reading would set a long-term patient brooding. But even though she was as persevering a Corkonian as her famous brother, she finally had to admit that rug-making was not my bag. And Sister Bruno, a dear, innocent, little, fat woman, elected to think that my literary activities concealed the identity of 'Nanky Poo' who wrote verses in *The Far East*, not a place but a periodical, and, for her sake, I was sorry they did not.

That Gilbertian pen-name partially concealed the identity of a learned and zealous cleric, a member of the missionary order, the Columban Fathers, who produced that magazine, and were intent on making good Irish Catholics out of the Chinese and in some, but comparatively few, instances, succeeding, perhaps. He was also related, in the flesh, to some elegant and eminent medical practitioners in my own town.

Those were eighteen happy months on the sun-balcony of Cappagh. Oh I knew what I was doing and why I was there and the place was real.

Finglas was all green fields then and, in the long evenings, the light died slowly over the Liffey valley and one had the leisure, and plenty of it, to get to know every detail of the opposing hills. Dublin was down there patiently awaiting my manifestation. But Dublin must be content, like myself, to wait. Also: What young fellow in the whole of his health, well except for the lump on the third lumbar, could object to being for eighteen months in the company of a regiment of handsome, good-natured nurses?

Then from the Christmas of 1939 until the following fall I was once again a part of Omagh Town, a small part, clad for a while in dark, clerical clothes but not really as sombre as they made me seem. The darkness of war was over the place, and over many another. Young Englishmen who had suddenly found themselves in the Royal Irish Fusiliers or the Inniskillings, the Skins, were being route-marched, most awkwardly, around the quiet byways of my boyhood. One day I watched and listened-to a platoon, or whatever, of them marching down the slope that led in from Enniskillen and Bundoran and the western ocean. They were singing that there would always be an England. Their singing was as awkward as their marching. They may have had sore feet. Anyway, a boozer is the place for singing. Not a cold, damp roadway in an alien town. They were young men torn away by war from home and on the road to God Knows Where!

A publican in the Town lamented to me that the world would never be the same again, that the military barracks contained nothing but Englishmen. Being a polite class of young fellow I had not the nerve to point out to him that it was, after all, a bloody British army barracks and Englishmen were entitled to enter.

There were a lot of Irishmen in there, too, and later on, and on far foreign fields, and some of them old friends of mine. Nor were they compelled nor conscripted.

But one notable parade I did witness during that brief revisit to the Town.

For one day I stood at Tom Kane's corner in John Street and watched those fusiliers, of the two varieties, marching off to France. All over again. At that corner, it seems to me, I have been forever standing, then, and before then, and since. The men who marched past at that moment seemed to me, young as I was, to be much too old and yellow in the face for a new and original war. For God's sake: they had already soldiered their way to India and back. And been for years working here and there, or simply leaning at the street-corners on what was described as the Reserve. Reserved for what?

But the Empire, in Omagh and elsewhere, had few other heroes to throw into the first line to stop the Wagnerians thundering towards us from the east. So off the yellow-faced men marched or were marched. They didn't look very pleased, as the warder in the Crumlin Road jail is said to have said, about the man he had but recently escorted, accompanied or assisted to the scaffold. Some of them, so as to get into fighting form again, had already been mixed into drunken brawls in the pubs and the fish-and-chippers. In one of which hassles one of the veterans of India had cracked an honest constable on the head with a tall, cylindrical, glass jar of hard confectionery. You don't see the like of those jars around any more. They must have been two feet in height and the glass walls were mighty thick. But in consideration of the place the offender was on his way to, the action for assault and battery, and obstructing, or whatever, a constable in the course of etcetera, was tucked away somewhere. And the constable recovered.

Rumours drifted back to the Town that before the breaker of glass jars and his comrades got as far as France they had to be interned, or coralled, for a while on the Isle of Wight. Where Alfred Lord Tennyson and others had been before them. They were so detained not by no means for mutiny but to give them a chance to sober up. So many years on the army-reserve of that time had given them a taste for gracious living.

At Kane's corner in John Street I, a ghostly figure, a revenant, stood and watched them pass. They were marching to France as, later in my narrative, you will find was, a long time ago but from the same place, the Comte d'Avaux. A man who seldom deserts my imagination.

But in the middle of the marching men, and a head above them all, marched Corker McCann, as fine a fighting man, in pub or on field of battle, as ever stood on two, or more, feet. And a voice in the crowd around me said: 'By Mars, if Corker McCann cannot stop the Germans the Maginot Line is banjaxed.'

Mars was not, although he had every right to be, the divinity referred to. Nor was the adjective used as polite as: banjaxed. Which is, anyway, a Dublinism of obscure linguistic origins.

*

And a few months after I watched that passing parade I arose and followed more-or-less in the direction the matching men had taken. But only got a bit of the way and never wore a uniform. Even if I had wanted to go into an army nobody, British or Irish, would have had me. And as for the other crowd I could neither speak nor spy in their language.

About the name of the Town you are about to visit. That is, if you feel up to the journey.

The use of the name Omey may require some elucidation for such of us as have not had the good fortune to come from that hallowed place.

In Rann na Feirsde, in the Rosses of Donegal, when a person would ask you where you came from he or she would say: 'Carbh as ċhú?'

Or, roughly: 'Where out of are you?'

And if you had the above-mentioned good fortune you would say, with pardonable pride: 'As an Oghmhaigh mé.'

Or: 'Out of the Omey I.'

Out of, that is, the verdant or virgin plain.

So in English you may call the place Omagh or the Omey as it pleases you or suits your palate.

There were, as in all such cases, coy jokes about the prevalence, or otherwise, of virginity and about the exceptional status, if that's the word, of the three black, winged women on the Boer War memorial that then ornamented the Courthouse hill. But was there ever a female figure on any monument anywhere in the world who was not similarly complimented?

ONE

The Entry

O magh Town, to the child, was what they called an Entry, off old Castle Street. The houses met over your head as you went into the Entry.

Torney McCrossan was the smartest lawyer, before Mr George Murnaghan, who ever stood up in the Courthouse. He had defended hundreds of people and, guilty or innocent, kept them off the gallows or out of Derry jail. He defended a woman. He told her to pretend she was mad. If she was asked a question she was to answer: 'Hoot Toot.' So she did that and went free down the Courthouse steps. When Torney McCrossan went to her for his fee she said: 'Hoot Toot.'

He made many enemies. That can happen to lawyers. One day he was walking out that Entry. From a window above somebody dropped a rope with a butcher's hook at the end of it and caught him under the chin and pulled him up. He was cleeked. That was what they called it: 'Torney McCrossan was cleeked.'

Clear of the archway, the Entry or laneway went down to something that the child liked to think of as a cliff, and the river was at the bottom of the cliff. Four houses on one side of the laneway, blank walls on the other. Granny Bradley lived in the first house and there was something about a row he had with her grandson, Harry, about a cocoa-tin or a pair of scissors or something.

There was a poem about the river:

Thrice happy and blessed were the days of my childhood,
And happy the hours I wandered from school
By Mountjoy's green forest, our dear native wildwood,
And the green flowery banks of the serpentine Strule.

He lived in the fourth house with his father and mother, two sisters
and one brother. Another sister was in Dublin. Another brother,
Macartan, who was eight, had died in the fever hospital. From a
relapse. He had diphtheria and he was better. But the nurses weren't
watching and Paddy Hunter and Macartan were up out of bed playing
in their shirts and bare feet on the cold flagstones of the floor: and
Macartan had his relapse. There was a picture of him in a dark gansey
and a great white collar, and with fair hair and big eyes. His mother
mentioned him again and again, but it isn't easy to see people clearly if
you were only three when they died.

You went out of the Entry into old Castle Street, which went up a
steep hill, and on the top of the hill the two spires went up to the sky.

McSorley's shop was where you turned the corner: and Jim McSorley
who had been a schoolteacher. He stood in the doorway of the shop,
and leaned on a stick, and shivered. He had been a schoolteacher until
the priest preached against the Republicans and Jim McSorley stood up
and walked out of the church: and then he was like that in the shopdoor.
So they said. But the child's sister, Kathleen, said they'd say anything:
and Kathleen and his brother, Gerry, and his father and mother and
Eileen paid no heed to what they said, and were always in the room
behind the shop talking to Cissy and Jim McSorley. Rita was in Dublin.

After that, the Town was another house and a place called the Hill,
and the Cow Commons, all chickweed: and Josie and Lanty who were
the child's first real friends in the Town. The Hill was Gallows Hill and
long ago men were hanged there and, by night, Adam Tait with his
head in his hand drove a black coach and four black horses over the top
of the Hill. Lanty had seen him. The Cow Commons was the slope of
the Hill, all men and cattle on a fairday. Lanty called it the Prairie.
Beyond the Cow Commons was the Big Field or Beacom's Field, and
the Station Brae and the railways to Belfast, Dublin, Enniskillen,
Bundoran, Derry. You could go to Bundoran on a Sunday for two
shillings and see the Atlantic ocean and come back home on the same
day.

From the front of the house you could look down into Hamilton's forge and the Back Alley where the Bonners lived who won the war, and over the forge and the Back Alley to the laundry chimney, the roofs of High Street and Market Street, the dome on the townhall, the county hospital on a hill above the Camowen river in the parish of Killyclogher or Cappagh.

Beyond all that were the mountains and Glenhordial where the water came from.

The Bonners won the war because so many of them joined the soldiers.

TWO

The Prayer at the Crossroads

There was a certain mystery about the journey, just for the day, back to the village of Dromore. It was made by road: a lift on a truck driven by his elder brother who was going there anyway to buy crates of eggs and fowls for the table, and great yellow miosgans of country-butter as big as rugby footballs and beaded with moisture from farmhouse churns: all for James Campbell of Knocknamoe Castle. Who was not a sufferer from diabetes nor yet possessed by the hunger demon. Nor did he need all that provender for his family, although he had six daughters and two sons and a gracious, brownhaired lady who was Mrs Campbell. And scores of men working for him around the Castle and in the town. And two hundred running greyhounds who ate beef and drank brandy.

No, James of Knocknamoe resold the produce in a place in John Street in the Town and in another place in Stockwell Street in Glasgow. After Stockwell Street he named a greyhound that became famous in the Waterloo Cup and was carried on a platform through the town in a torchlight procession with St Eugene's brass-and-reed band marching in front and Red Dan McCrory beating the big drum: a man who, in reality, once sawed away the branch of a tree he was sitting on and broke a leg when he hit the ground. Protestant and Catholic, Orange and Green, rich and poor, marched together, singing and cheering, in that torchlight procession, and his father said that it might be the will of God that a greyhound would unite Ireland.

23

It was also said that James of Knocknamoe sold white turkeys at Christmas to the Royal family.

It was ten miles from the Town to the village. Past the Flush where the stream burst out from the fields and ran beside the road, sometimes flooding it. Over the Creevan burn at Cavanacaw schoolhouse, then through the long Clanabogan plantation. In the middle of the plantation were the Protestant church and the haunted crossroads. His mother remembered that when the church was being topped by the steeple the minister of the time asked a labouring man could he guess the height the steeple would be. 'Like your sermons, the height of nonsense,' the man said. And had the sack for his wit or candour.

Down that side road, and much surpassing the entourage of Adam Tait on Gallows Hill, comes exactly on the stroke of midnight the ghostly hearse with headless horses and headless driver: real living horses have been known to rust and stall in terror at that place at that time. One night of wind and rain the brother is driving a half-ton Ford truck, known affectionately as the Wee Green and loaded with crates of raucous fowl, past that crossroads and gateway. The clock in the steeple strikes midnight. The truck breaks down. So the brother sends his helper, Willy Lowe, back fifty yards to Clanabogan post office to rouse the postmaster and ring the Town for help: and sits himself to wait and watch the truck and the cargo. But the roof of the cab of the truck is leaking and, to find shelter, he climbs the wall of the churchyard and lies down on a grave and under an ancient table-tombstone: where Willy Lowe, the helping-man, swears to God he finds him, quite at his ease, when he returns. 'Real nice quiet people in Clanabogan,' the brother said. 'Not one of them said a word to me.'

He has a quiet, iron nerve and a dry humour. Best man ever to sing, for the hell of it, bel-canto after the fashion of Amelita Galli-Curchi: 'A gipsy coming through a meadow, spied a bir-ir-ird up-ohon a tree, Tra-la-la-la-la-la . . .' which he sings this morning, the sun shining, the leaves of the plantation all light green for Spring, and not a headless monster anywhere to be seen.

That road to the right to Bundoran and the Atlantic ocean, passing on the way all the beauty of Loch Erne with an island for every day in the year, and the Boa island where, the child's mother says, young people dance in the evenings on platforms at the crossroads: and the Stone

Fiddle of Castlecauldwell, and some day his father, who knows the place well, will tell him the story about why the Stone Fiddle is there and about the fiddler that was drowned drunk in the Loch two hundred years ago.

But we take the road to the left with nothing much to pass but Shaneragh creamery, and the Shaneragh or the Blacksessiagh river which is one part of the bigger river that flows through the Town: and come to the small town or village of Dromore where his mother and his brother and Willy Lowe and himself eat a meal in an eating-house: and then his mother and himself set off to walk to The House: and this is where the mystery comes in. The House is the house he was born in on 15 August 1919, an easy date to remember and a day off from school because it is the feast of the Assumption and also, his mother says, the birthday of St John Bosco and of Fr John Drumgoole who founded orphanages in the United States, and also, as he is later to find out, of Walter Scott, Napoleon Bonaparte, and others.

The man who now lives in The House is John McPeake. The House is the best part of two miles away, so off they set to walk, while the brother and Willy Lowe are left to buy eggs and fowl for the table, and rabbits even, and all the rest of it.

His mother and himself come to the crossroads: well not exactly a crossroads, only three roads, not four, the road they are walking on, another road that goes straight ahead, dipping and rising, to the town of Fintona: and a road that swings right to Enniskillen and Trillick and The House. At that sort of crossroads his mother takes out her rosary-beads and kneels down and tells him to do likewise, and she leads and he answers one Our Father, three Hail Marys and one Glory Be, and she says: 'Eternal rest grant unto them, O Lord, and let thy perpetual light shine upon them. May they rest in peace, Amen.'

They walk on. She says: 'Three men died there. Your father knew them.'

A little later she says: 'God break a hard fate. Protect all sinners from the unfortunate hour.'

And before they come to The House there is another house to visit. To the right of the road. Up a long avenue lined with trees. A big, white, two-storeyed house, and people fussing and coming and going, and a man sitting in bed in the middle of the day in a grey nightshirt and a nightcap, a thin man, not shaven, a sad quiet sort of man. This man is his godfather, Joe Corey: he has been called Thomas after his father, Benedict after the Pope and Joseph after the man in the nightshirt who stood up for him, his mother says, at the baptismal font and at the throne of God. They all drink tea and talk. The sun is on the garden outside but the room is dim and there is something in it, not exactly a smell.

In the Easter week of 1916 a beggarwoman called Nan the Rat had come into The House and told the child's mother that the rebels had entered the town of Strabane with fixed bayonets. His brother, who was then eight years of age, heard her. It was an innocent world and the brother wasn't quite sure what a bayonet was. But he felt sorry for the rebels who could not afford good new bayonets and had to make do with things fixed-up with string or rags or whatever. About the same time the first aeroplane flew over, and the brother and all his pals ran in terror and hid under appletrees and currant bushes. Later still, and at the railway-station across the meadow from The House, the train was held up and the mails robbed, and shots fired, and a bullet went through a dormer window: and Gyp, the dog, vanished that night and came back a week later running wild with joy to be home again. It was thought that the dog had been doped and kidnapped to keep him from barking on the night of the raid. The child never met Gyp the dog, only heard of him. He didn't notice much about John McPeake: just a name to be remembered.

That summer after the visit the man in the grey nightshirt died. Willy Lowe said they took him to the county hospital and opened him and took a look and, when they saw what they saw, they sewed him up again and sent him home: not a hope.

Did the death of the man in the grey nightshirt mean that now he had nobody to stand up for him before the throne of God?

The three men who had been prayed for at the crossroads had been dragged out of their homes and murdered by the Specials: a sort of Orange yeomanry or Bashi-Bazouk (See: Bernard Shaw), set up to defend the northeast corner of Ireland against the Pope and Eamonn de Valera. All this he is to hear about and half-comprehend a long time afterwards. The three may or may not have been members of the IRA of the time: 1920. Then it was said that no man who had hand, act or part in the Dromore murders would ever die in his bed. Instances were cited. A curious fanatical clergyman who died in a road-accident and thereafter haunted the place he died at: to the no small discomfiture of horsemen passing by. And the man who was found dead in the manhole when the flood subsided. This was how that happened.

Right in the heart of the Town the rivers Drumragh and Camowen met to form the Strule:

> Hair of my head, two locks I offer. This to Inachus,
> River of home who nursed my childhood.

In rainy seasons the confluence was most constipated and the waters could rise to two feet or more on the streets, Campsie Avenue or Campsie Crescent: and this man, and many said he had been a Dromore murderer, was wading home through the flood, and the water had lifted a manhole cover and, when the flood subsided, there he was in the manhole with his neck broken.

There was the celebrated and, after a fashion, comic case of Wee Tom Briscoe, a merchant in the Town: a tiny, inoffensive man and not at all unpopular. But the rumour was that he had been standing by when the dirty deed was done: and the more credulous section of a section of his fellow countrymen, and women, observed his career with scientific interest. Then sometime in the 1940s, and a long time after the day when those prayers were said at the crossroads, Wee Tom was persuaded to stand as Unionist candidate for that part of the world and for the deliberative assemblies at Stormont and Westminster.

To address the crowd on the slope of High Street and below the great Courthouse in the Town, the Nationalists brought from the far west of Connacht a man who, in the deliberative assembly in Leinster House, Kildare Street, Dublin, represented an acreage of the wide plains of Mayo. Which was a fine idea, except that the Mayoman had not done his homework nor listened too carefully to his briefing. Nor did he seem quite certain as to what part of Ireland he happened at that moment to be in. It was possible to suspect that on the way from Mayo to the Town he may have sipped some stimulants: perhaps even have spoken to Big Tom Reilly who had once been a famous footballer for the County Cavan. So, standing on a platform below the Doric columns of the Courthouse and waving in his hand some sheets of Unionist publicity or

propaganda or something, he kept roaring such Ciceronian provoca-
tions as: 'Our opponent, Big Tom says . . . But I will controvert Big
Tom and, here and now, tell Big Tom to his teeth that . . .'

Seated modestly out of sight in a lawyer's office on the Courthouse
Hill Wee Tom listened to the reshaping of his image and, after a long
time, said to two legal friends who sat there with him, Captain Fyffe, a
Unionist, George Rodgers, a Nationalist: 'Jasus knows, Captain and
George, I've been called many's the thing in my time, but I was never
called Big Tom before this day.'

George was the elder and one and only brother of Josie who had
walked the Hill with himself and Lanty, who had seen Adam Tait.

Big James of Knocknamoe did not like to stay in the Castle on his own
when the family was away. It was high on a hill with tall trees all around
it: and it had a closed room with a ghost in it. So the brother stayed with
him for company and Big James said to the father, describing the
breakfasts the brother and himself had in Knocknamoe: 'Gerry's a
bloody good chef.'

The mother was much amused. She said: 'James of Knocknamoe is
easy pleased. Gerald can boil eggs and brew tea.'

She never said Gerry.

In the 1960s it was that Knocknamoe became an hotel. The
Americans were there during the Hitler war. It was even said that,
coming up to D-day, Eisenhower and Monty and others met in an oak-
panelled room in the Castle. The panelling in Knocknamoe was
beautiful. But when the owner of the hotel asked the British War Office
to verify the story of that meeting, they were too mean to say yes or no.
The owner thought the detail might interest tourists. Perhaps it was just
as well that the War Office did not respond. Things turned out to be bad
enough as they were. For in the bloody 1970s, the Destabilisers, the
creators of Éire Núa (the New Ireland), planted a bomb there and
destroyed the panelling and killed three British soldiers. An eminent
Dublin journalist was in the hotel that night. The blast blew him out of
his bed. He said that the bits of one of the soldiers were in the branches
of a tree: not too far from the Killyclogher Burn where long ago my
brother and myself, and many another, used to fish. All that, I
mentioned to the brother. He said thoughtfully: 'I knew more about
Knocknamoe than anybody else.'

I agreed: 'You stayed there nights with Big James to keep the ghost locked in the room.'

'No, I don't mean that. You know the Boundary Commission met in Knocknamoe: the fake piece of window-dressing that the British set up when they decided to partition Ireland.'

'I know.'

'There were old maps lying in Knocknamoe that the Boundary Commission left behind it when the farce folded. One of them showed that it was planned to give the Lagan to the Belfast puppet government and the Orangemen. Not the Lagan river . . .'

'I know.'

'They had that already. But all the fertile land in East Donegal on the far side of the Foyle water. Dublin, or the so-called Free State, was to be fobbed off with a bit of scrubland at the backside of Fermanagh. Over in London Lloyd George the Welsh Wizard was cocking his thumb at us. Sealed envelope. Immediate and terrible war. And I saw the corpses in the ditch after the Dromore murders. They were in a bad way. They were friends of your father. You were a year old at the time.'

Some time in the late 1960s the youngest of the three sisters said to me when I was on a visit to the Town: 'Your friend, Tom Briscoe, died last week.'

For over the years, and because of George Rodgers, he had become friendly with Wee Tom. So I said: 'Did he die in his bed?'

'No,' she says, 'in the chair beside the bed.'

That the prophecy might be fulfilled.

THREE

Days of Bands and Ballads

Round about 1929 I began to realise that He was Me.

Music, for most of us, may begin with the mother singing: and poetry, perhaps, with the father reciting. Or it could be the other way around. Or it could be that you come from one of those favoured households in which father and mother both sang and recited. My sorrow for you if your father and mother did neither one nor the other, even if they may have done their best to compensate by being rich.

In my own case my mother sang and my father recited, although my father could so far forget his station in life as, on occasion, to sing 'The Captain with the Whiskers': a song that pursues me still. The only other person I ever heard sing it properly was that lovely woman, Nuala MacDonagh, wife of the poet, Donagh MacDonagh who was son to that other poet, Thomas, who died in 1916.

My father also sang, I am sorry to say, the complete and unexpurgated opus of 'Doran's Ass', which begins fairly and politely enough with the statement that Paddy Doyle lived in Killarney and loved a maid named Betsy Toole, but goes on to psychodelic matters outside the experience of the new middle-class. He could also sing about the Donegal migratory labourers, the tatie-howkers, sailing down the Broomielaw on their way home from the Scottish potato-harvest:

> Wha saw the tatie-howkers,
> Wha saw them gang awa,

30

Wha saw the tatie-howkers
Sailing doon the Broomielaw?
Some of them wore bits and stockings,
Some of them wore nane ata,
Some of them wore bits and stockings,
Sailing doon the Broomielaw.

Then carefully he would annotate: and explain about the woeful hardship of the lives of those labourers, and how they had been written about in the novels, *Children of the Dead End* and *The Rat-Pit*, by Patrick MacGill from Glenties in the County Donegal, whom your mother knew when he was a labouring-boy in Young's of the Hollow near Drumquin. The father had himself been born in Donegal, in the seaside town of Moville and, oddly enough, in the barracks of the then Royal Irish Constabulary.

But apart from those few songs, and some other detached fragments, recitation was really his bag, and on at least one night of every week the Chieftain to the Highlands bound passed through our house, drawing breath for a while to implore the boatman not to tarry: or the sun was low on Hohenlinden: or around the fire one winter's night the farmer's rosy children sat and the knock came to the door and in, out of the tempest, came the travelling-man:

Cold blows the blast across the moor,
The dreary moor that I have passed.

The songs, too, brought with them their own people who, like the captain with the whiskers, became part of my life and have stayed with me.

Ireland, when I hum old songs to myself, is still Ireland through joy and through tears, a most abstract idea, and hope never dies through the long weary years: which may be very true and, in these times, very necessary. Dennis Cox, whom I met in 1945 or 1946 on the boat to Greenock where he was going to sing at a Patrick's Day concert, had made a Parlophone red-label record (disc) of that song. At that meeting with Dennis Cox I, for the sweet irony of it, was going to the Central Hotel in Sauchiehall Street, Glasgow, to give a lecture to the Glasgow Irish National Association on the origins and implications of the partition of Ireland: about which, so help me God, I had just written a

book, my first, called *Counties of Contention*. That was the age of
romantic innocence.

But, happily far away from national sentiment on the grand scale, the
unknown man who wrote 'The True Lovers' Discourse' still for me
plays Peeping or Listening Tom on the other side of the hedge.
Margaret O'Reilly, the ballad-singing woman from the shores of Loch
Gowna in the County Cavan, has most of the words of that song which
was so long, as my mother once told me, that a man driving a horse and
cart over the Barrack Hill in Omagh Town began to sing it and was still
singing, without having repeated a verse, eight miles away at Segully
Crossroads:

> This couple spoke with such voice of reason,
> Their sentiments they expressed so clear,
> That for to listen to their conversation
> My inclination was to draw near . . .

The well-dressed gentleman who was passing by still makes his
advances to the maid in the lonely garden, offering her a high, high
building and a castle fine and a ship on the ocean: and the Cork girl
lamenting by the Owenabwee, the yellow river, where it flows towards
Drake's pool, still swears to follow Dark Domhnall to wear the *fleur de
lys* on the battlefields of France: and the roses bloom again down by yon
river and the robin redbreast sings his sweet refrain.

The song was valued for the words; the ballad for the new people it
brought into your life and for the story it told: and all that, as we all
know, is very far away from the appreciation of music. Yet the music
kept echoing in the mind and made the words more memorable.

For public performances of music in the days of my boyhood there were
parochial concerts at which lady doctors from Derry City sang about the
merry, merry pipes of Pan. Derry people, we were assured, were very
musical. Our parish priest, John McShane, a learned doctor of the Irish
College in Rome who had met D'Annunzio and who spoke from the
pulpit about *Hibernia Irredenta*, meaning the Six Counties, also came
from Derry: it was even said that he went back to Derry to have his hair
cut.

At those concerts, too, serious and pallid young ladies, in royal-blue gansies and navy-blue pleated skirts, from the Loreto convent, danced Irish dances and played the violin with what Brendan Behan used to call great function. They were good at the violin. Like the decent Dublin girl said in Hatch Street, Dublin, and about something else altogether and on the night before the cattlemarket, they had medals to prove it: in the dubious dark it would seem that some ungrateful client had slipped her two holy medals instead of two halfcrowns. But faraway as Tophet from all that were the blue Loreto dancers. They performed, also, in plays, but the appearance and also, possibly, the excitation of long male pants for male parts (roles), created problems of morality and the giving of scandal. By the ukase of the Reverend Mother, pants of that sort were forbidden and, for a performance of Patrick Pearse's mystical-patriotic play, *The Singer*, ('One man can save a people as one man redeemed the world'), MacDara, the singer, played by a strong-voiced and strong-bodied girl from Fintona, had his or her cross-gartered calves and thighs multiply swathed in sacking in a way that would have excited comment in Outer Mongolia.

At one of those concerts at the age of ten I made my first stage-appearance, reciting word-perfect, and the hell terrified out of me by my teacher, Brother J. D. Hamill, Florence M. Wilson's long poem about Thomas Russell, friend of Robert Emmet who for his patriotism was hanged at Downpatrick jail in 1803. As Emmet had been dealt with in Dublin a little earlier.

> By Downpatrick jail I was bound to fare
> On a day I'll remember, feth,
> For when I came to the prison square,
> The people were gathered in hundreds there
> And you wouldn't hear stir nor breath.
> For the soldiers were standing grim and tall,
> Round a scaffold built there fornenst the wall,
> And a man stepped out for death.

As is only proper I quote, after sixty years, or misquote, from memory. The performer who preceded me was a lady-doctor from Derry City and she did sing about the merry, merry pipes of Pan.

But for the untutored ear the important musical event in the town was the marching forth of the bands. They were St Eugene's brass and reed band and the two splendidly caparisoned bands, one brass and one pipes, of the Fusiliers. A farmer in the vicinity of the town had a reputation for leaving the furrow half-ploughed, or the stook half-tied, so that he could follow his fancy and the brass-bands. Then there was Paddy Woods's pipe band, a fine and private enterprise but somewhat halting in actual performance. On one public occasion when Paddy was asked if his troupe could manage the national anthem, not the King but the Soldiers' Song, he modestly answered: 'Every second note.'

There were also the several Orange bands: fifes and pipes. Those absurd accordion bands, resembling nothing so much as a lot of ladies marching along with their knitting, and which, television tells me, are even to be found in Tibet, had not yet been either thought of or tolerated. But the Orange bands were different because, except for a few occasions in the year, they performed only in the Orange Hall and, even when out in the open air, their principal concern was not the making of music. They had their political axe to grind, and grind it they did to the detriment of all eardrums and, sometimes, even with the help of the Killyman Rattlers, a battalion of Lambeg big-drummers from East Tyrone who sounded like thunder after forked lightning, louder but much more musical than any modern disco.

Sunday morning was the big time for the real bands. There seemed to be a quiet understanding between St Eugene's and the imperial bands that one Sunday would be civilian and the next Sunday military. If you were an RC in the British army, and in Omagh barracks at that time the majority of the Skins and the Royal Irish probably were, one good reason for getting up early and going to first Mass was that you might dodge church-parade. Was the OC as cunning as a Jesuit or was it, simply, that Ignatius of Loyola was a soldier: a sanctified sergeant-major, Francis Thompson said. For while the parade might be a sight for idle civilians it was a sore Sunday drag for the soldiers: spit and polish and a stiff march up old Castle Street, the blare of the brass rattling the window-frames, and prayers on top of that, and a sermon. Join the army and see the world, how are you?

Then for an hour or more after last Mass and weather permitting, and it often permitted, the band of the day gave a recital on a sort of terrace before the parish church. Harvests may have gone ungathered and Sunday meals been burned to cinders. The people were hungry for music. That terrace has long since been cut away for the convenience of trucks and lesser automobiles, and bandsmen nowadays would need also to be mountain goats, or rolling stones, to perform on the slope that remains. But then people nowadays have other ways of getting their music and cooking the meal at the same time.

Bands and country-ballads and sentimental drawing-room songs! But then in secret corners were the real men, clutching their mysteries, small groups of them like groups of college students going on marijuana trips, hoarding their collections of classical records, dark-label Columbia or HMV, guarding them from scratch and dust and the defiling touch of the ignorant or infidel. Friendships were shattered over a record carelessly scratched.

It was my luck that one of this elect should take the notion to marry one of my sisters, and should then go ahead and do so. He was a Shavian and a Wellsian and a man who could, and can, play everything from the cello to the ocarina. One of his spare-time activities was the training of St Eugene's brass-and-reed band. In the town of Strabane, twenty miles to the north and downstream, they tried to go one better by setting up a silver band. Strabane people were never content.

That Shavian brother-in-law taught my brother to play the clarinet: no mean achievement in the teaching of music, as my brother was prepared to admit. The first tune taught and learned was *Eibhlinn Arúin*, the ancient haunting melody that has, to go with it, ancient Irish words that were dressed up in English in the nineteenth century by Gerald Griffin in a version much admired by Lord Tennyson. Eileen was the name of the relevant sister. It was courting by clarinet and by proxy. Also: he tried to teach me to play the fiddle but I failed him for reasons that had more to do with perverted snobbery than with inability to bow and finger. The loafers who held up Kane's corner, which I had to pass on my way to music lessons, were inclined to whistle and make remarks and other nasty noises when a little boy passed with a violin case, and I hadn't the moral backbone to brave them. To tell the God's truth my heart was with the loafers. Plain blunt people may be a little afraid of formal music. But I have lived to regret that failure. Every man, barbarian or civilised, should play at least one musical instrument. And have a trade: cobbling or carpentry or whatever. Something useful.

My brother-in-law's chief fellow-classicist at that time was an atheistical postman who later in life was to meet his bride-to-be in the back of a truck on the road to Brest and after the battle of Dunkirk: I will have cause to mention him again. Together these two fanatics would play instruments or recordings or talk about this and that: God or Gluck or George Gissing. In a corner that was part of their secret corner I sat and listened, feeling the way I still feel in the secret world of great music. Swept away and lost and overwhelmed, but struggling to understand.

FOUR

Three Barbers and Freney the Robber

The first haircut I ever had in public, that is in a barber's shop, cost my father twopence. It was fourpence for adults and half price for wee fellows and the time was some time before 1929. That barber, long dead and gone to God, was a quiet, Godfearing man but had for a brother that atheistical postman, already mentioned, who was also on the reserve of the Royal Air Force. He it was who, in 1940, in the course of the retreat to and from Dunkirk, met that French girl in the back of a truck and married her, though not, I suspect, in the truck: and brought her back to the Home Town to the amazement of all. Few men did so well out of the battle of Dunkirk.

What I remember most of all about that haircut was the man who sat in the chair next to me: the only other occupied chair in the shop at the time. He was a big man with long legs and one of the biggest sets of feet, the regulation two of them, that I have ever seen. He talked in a highfalutin' sort of a voice, and he and the barber were obviously great friends and, when he was clipped and trimmed and all, he gave the barber a five-pound note and took no change. That was big money before 1929 and at a time when an ordinary haircut cost fourpence. How I even knew it was a fiver was, of course, because of the brother and the buying in the markets for Big James of Knocknamoe. Carefully I had observed him when he was doing his accounts so that I knew what all denominations of big money, from fives to fifties and sometimes above, looked like. Cheques were not all that common then, nor for a long time afterwards, nor all that welcome, in the North of Ireland: a reflection of the canny Scottish influence.

Afterwards I found out that the man with the big feet was a belted bloody earl who always came there to be shorn (his estates were thirty miles away), just because he liked the barber, and who never restricted his payment to fourpence: and I developed a high opinion of earls.

Along the street in which I had that first haircut there was another barber who was a renowned soccer footballer: and I knew a barber, a fine young man too, in the pleasant city of Eugene, Oregon, who read the Bible most of the time in the shop when he wasn't barbering, so that when he closed the book and advanced upon you with comb and shears and scissors you were given to wondering what text, at that moment, was revolving in his head. At first I thought, somewhat nervously, that he might be a religious maniac but then I discovered that he was merely a student for the ministry at a nearby Bible college, or seminary.

Yet I never knew a barber who in his spare time was a highwayman, as a certain Irish lady of the eighteenth to nineteenth century did, and as she so recorded in her journals. This is what the lady wrote:

> The roads in many places were almost impassable in wet weather and the great robber was always on the alert to stop passengers. But as he was a native of Inistioge he was known to have lain down in a ditch to let Lady Betty Ferguson pass by unalarmed. . . . He began life as a servant, and while dressing his master's hair at Woodstock told him of a robbery which had been committed the night before, his master little suspecting that he, i.e., the servant, had been the robber himself and had returned to the house in time to dress him.

The great robber was Captain Freney, no more a captain than yourself and myself, who harassed the roads of the southeast of Ireland in the early nineteenth century and about whom P. J. McCall wrote a good ballad:

> I met Captain Freney beyond Monasterevan,
> Dark night in his pistols, bright day in his eye,
> But he seemed out of sorts, for says he, 'Tommy Devin,
> Did you see the King's man with his bags riding by.'

The fragment of information that I quoted about him just now was written down by Caroline Tighe of the notable Tighe family of Woodstock House, the ruins of which, burned-out in the *jacquerie* of the 1920s, may be seen high above the river Nore and the beautiful little town of Inistioge in the County Kilkenny. The family may have been responsible for introducing the novelist Charles Lever to the beauties of Inistioge, which he describes in detail in the novel A *Day's Ride*: and, by way of another house they had in Ashford, County Wicklow, introducing the poet, Thomas Moore, to the beauties of the Vale of Avoca in whose bosom the bright waters still manage to meet: in spite of copper mines and nitrogen plants. Caroline's comment on Freney I found in a history of the family compiled for the use of the family by the late Admiral W. G. S. Tighe.

There were many more people in that history than Freney, the barber and robber. There was that delicate poetess, Mary Tighe, who died, from a decline and an unhappy marriage, in 1810 at the age of thirty-eight. Keats may have read her with pleasure. Thomas Moore wrote a poem to her:

> Though many a gifted mind we meet,
> Though fairest forms we see,
> To live with them is far less sweet
> Than to remember thee, Mary . . .

She came to be known as Psyche Tighe because she wrote in the Spenserian stanza a long poem about love and the marriage of Cupid and Psyche:

> Now through the hall melodious music stole,
> And self-prepared the splendid banquet stands,
> Self-poured the nectar sparkles in the bowl,
> The lute and viol touched by unseen hands
> Aid the soft voices of the choral bands;
> O'er the full board a brighter lustre beams
> Than Persia's monarch at his feast commands:
> For sweet refreshment all inviting seems
> To taste celestial food, and pure ambrosial streams.

One stanza there out of three hundred and sixty-two: a fluent footnote to Apuleius from Africa.

And Felicia Hemans, who is buried in the vaults of St Ann's Church in Dawson Street in Dublin, and who wrote about that heat-resistant boy who stood on the burning-deck, also wrote about the grave of Mary Tighe:

> I stood beside thy lowly grave
> Spring odours breathed around,
> And music, in the river wave,
> Passed with a lulling sound.

And so on in the best style of that poetess of the affections who in her time was immensely popular with everybody except her husband: who bolted. Unlike the uninflammable boy.

Back by the *commodius vicus* of recirculation to John Street, Omagh, and my first barber, and that godless brother of his and his French wife, the spoils of war. The barber's wife was a quiet, pious Irishwoman who every morning walked home with my mother from eight o'clock Mass, and modestly accepted a cup of tea and seldom, in conversation, went beyond mildly-curious queries about the neighbours or sighing plaints about the sad state of the world. But one morning she was provoked to eloquence: 'That Frenchwoman,' she said, 'I'll tell you something about that Frenchwoman. She's so careful that when she cuts a slice off a pan-loaf she locks it up immediately and the crumbs with it. She wouldn't feed the birds.'

But in the unbelieving husband of that woman from somewhere in the Auvergne, whose saving habits were overmuch even for a Scotified Ulster, the stage, it may be, lost a superb entertainer. He was well content with his woman. No better man ever, not even Bransby Williams, who was then to be found doing it on black-label Columbia, to recite, 'The Green Eye of the Little Yellow God'. A small man, of much vitality and merriment he did, as sure as God, believe in music. In matters theological, or perhaps untheological, he came only second-in-command to the town's chief unbeliever, a jeweller, a tall man distinguished in style, learning and appearance. He was what we then called a returned American: meaning an Irishman who had spent a long time in the United States and then returned to settle in the land of his birth. Most returned Americans were well-to-do farmers. Jewellers, among them, were rare.

On Sunday afternoons and in the long summer evenings he strode impressively on the roads around the town, swinging a splendid gold-topped walking-stick, officer-class, three or four Irish setters trotting at his heels. On the far side of the Atlantic he had studied precious stones, and Time and the gadgets that marked it: and, there also, developed his ideas on Eternity and the Man who ruled it. He was generally regarded with awe and, oddly enough, with reverence.

On one Good Friday a handsome young woman, Ita, called into his shop to leave a clock for mending. Because of the day it was, no bell was rung from the high spires, not even the knell that tolled for mortals. The death of God was marked by silence, and statues and even golden crucifixes draped in cloth of dark purple.

Not only was Ita handsome but she had a beautiful soprano voice and her *Adeste* on a Christmas morning was worth rising early and travelling far to hear. Always a great friend of my mother, she was to become a great friend of my own and, years afterwards, she told me of that conversation on a Good Friday with the jeweller who was skilled to speak of time and eternity.

'Ita,' he said, 'you are off now to attend the special Good Friday devotions in the big house on the top of Church Hill.'

She admitted that she was. She said in jest: 'Won't you come with me.'

'No,' he said. 'No. I could not enter the house of a Man . . . I am not talking now of John McShane, a good man according to his lights but merely the caretaker of the house on the top of Church Hill . . . no, I could never bring myself to enter the house of a Man who, if I offended him, would treat me worse than I would treat my dogs.'

She was, she told me, then so young and simple that it took her a long time working out who the man was that he was talking about.

FIVE

Meditations on a Metal Bridge

For the purpose of these meditations the year is 1980 and I am revisiting the Town for a few days: forty-three years after I resigned from the position of regular resident.

The house in which my hostess lives and in which, as a consequence, I am a guest is on the edge of a steep slope above the Drumragh river: so-called here because before it enters the Town to join another river and lose its identity it flows through the townland of Drumragh. Rich agricultural land. Strong presbyterian farmers.

From where I stand in this house I can look down on the river and on the Linn Bridge, a metal bridge that once carried across the deep narrow water the railway to Portadown and intermediate stations, and then to Dublin or Belfast depending on your choice or mission. It no longer carries a railway: the line was abolished, like the Harcourt Street line in Dublin and many another elsewhere, and the fine stone station-buildings allowed to decay: an act of silent destruction that happened long before destruction in these parts became noisy and demonstrative. Destruction is always abominable, but once upon a time it seemed to be half-ashamed of itself. Not so any longer.

The Linn Bridge had in my boyhood as important a place in the business of proving something as has the ascent of Everest in the lives of men with higher ambitions. Foot-travellers could cross it by plank-platforms on both sides of the permanent way. That was two feet down on a bed of metal which clanked and boomed when a train passed. It took nerve to stand on one of the platforms and outface a passing train. But the real test was to step down to that metal bed (when no train was expected: naturally), open a trapdoor, clamber ten or twelve feet down a straight metal ladder to a three-plank-wide catwalk used by repair and maintenance men: then out and up along a stone ledge and so back, from outside, on to the bridge.

Below you was the still, deep pool (Linn) that gave the bridge its name. If you survived that operation then you were a man, my son, but the memory of it recurred in many youthful nightmares.

One sunny day about 1932 there were three boys and a Christian Brother on that bridge: the great Brother J. D. Hamill who was also brother in the flesh to Mickey Hamill, one of the great soccer centrehalfs of the 1920s. In Belfast on the Falls Road and in his retirement from football, Mickey had a pub called, it had to be, the Centrehalf: I met him once and in the presence of his reverend brother, J. D., shook his hand. I also once met Dixie Dean and Jack Dempsey. So shake the hand that . . .

Howandever: J. D. Hamill was opening the trapdoor when a train came thundering down from the direction of Sixmilecross. Tommy Cunningham, a schoolfellow of mine, panicked and shouted: 'Jump, you bloody fool, jump.'

J. D., at his ease, lowered the trapdoor, dusted his hands, stepped up to the platform. It was a lesson in nerve-control: as one day in the classroom he allowed a wasp to crawl all over his face to show us that no wasp would sting you if you left it alone. He didn't bother about being called, by one of his students, a bloody fool. He always said that there was no bad language, only language and strong language and dirty language. He had been in China and spoke Chinese.

That dread dark pool there below the bridge had a bad name for drownings. It had even claimed the life of Long Alec Nixon, a strong swimmer on whom in some unfortunate moment the treacherous current played one of its quiet tricks. For days they dragged the deep water for Alec: and from a steep slope, over there to my left and a sort of a natural grandstand, the people silently watched. One of themselves, a popular man, was down there, taken away by the river that was always with them and had never said a word. Children, myself among them, played on the green bank and were aware that something exciting was going on. Dragging the river: it sounded like the name of a new game.

Greater excitement, even a better game, during the Great Northern Railway strike in the 1930s when a train coming from Belfast was derailed at the bridge. The exact date I cannot recall: there was another derailment at the time, somewhere near Dundalk. When a train crossed that bridge, down there below me now in the sunshine, it had, if it was going into the Town, a choice: to the left to the main station, to the right to an auxiliary goods-station by the market-yard. So somebody pulled out an iron bar at the parting of the ways and the train went up the embankment between the two lines. The result was most impressive: nobody was seriously injured but carriages were tossed about like matchsticks. Half the Town, it was said, knew who had pulled out the bar: his name was frequently mentioned. But nobody talked officially: the strike had turned nasty and it was accepted that the men had just cause, and that was that. There was a man in the Town, an import though from Portadown or some foreign place, who for long after and until he moved off elsewhere was known, not unamiably, as Blank the Blackleg. Blank was not his real name.

We did not realise it at the time but that was the first instance that most of us had ever seen of violence and destruction. The general opinion then was that the railway-men, as against the company, were well justified. Being of a garrison town we had heard tall and other stories about the Western Front and about how Jerry couldn't face the cold steel: and when I studied the old-style bayonet, and gave the matter some thought, I came to the conclusion that the Germans were an eminently sensible people. We had heard of those Dromore murders that had happened, as I've noted, when I was a year old, and had happened a mile away from the house I was born in, and we hoped, and fondly thought that such things neither would nor could happen again.

There was trouble in Belfast in 1935. There was even an incident seven miles away from us in the small town of Fintona but it was caused by unwise men from the east, (i.e. Belfast), and one wild woman with the west in her eyes: and settled, how I cannot recall, in our own great Doric Courthouse on the top of the hill. Trouble in those days was mainly confined to that one spot in Belfast where the Shankill almost met, but mingled not, with the Falls. But that vision of the railway carriages tossed here and there was, looking back on it, a sort of mild introduction to the world we now live in. People preserved the newspaper clippings for years.

All below me now in the sunshine: the river, the great rolling fields, the track where the railway once did run, and one man and his dog walking along it. Omagh Town is built on hills. Gabriel Fallon, the Dublin theatre critic, and Abbey actor of the early days, who was up here years ago adjudicating an amateur drama festival, was the first man to draw my attention to the mountainous nature of my native place. Having been reared here, I hadn't noticed. Many other things you don't notice when you grow up. Were the blossoming bushes always as splendid as they now are all around me in this suburb on the Dublin road? Or have the laburnum and lilac and mock-orange of the Dublin suburbs simply made me more aware of blossoming bushes? Similarly: some years ago on Donnelly's bridge over the Camowen river on the Killyclogher road I marvelled at the moans and multiplicity of the wood-pigeons in the riverside trees. Had they been so plentiful there when I was young? Or had the woods around Emo in the County Laois, where I was from the spring of 1937 to the spring of 1938, merely made me hypersensitive to the existence of wood-pigeons?

The man and the dog have disappeared and the world is empty. Beyond the old railway track are the high trees along the Crevenagh road, once, and perhaps still, a famous Lovers' Lane, for serious lovers, not for dilettantes or amateurs. The Killyclogher road might then have been for wooing and light laughter, the Crevenagh road spelled action. No young lady, zealous for her reputation, would wish to be seen too often walking there.

But even that reflection dates me as an Edwardian, or worse. The motorcar must have made all that secret walking unnecessary: and holidays in Torremolinos. Far from Torremolinos were we reared. The best we could manage was Bundoran when the Scottish girls were there but, even then, all Omagh was there before you and attentive to your every move.

At the wide window above the river and the metal bridge I thumb through a file of a small excellently-produced magazine called *Pace*.

An article herein recalls me brutally to the present moment and reminds me, if any reminder is necessary, that life in the North is not all

fond memories and blossoming bushes, and sunlight on fields, and a
river loved since childhood. Dr H. A. Lyons of the Purdsyburn Hospital
in Belfast is writing about the legacy of violence:

> Therefore, when peace comes, it is to be anticipated that there will be
> an increase in general criminal behaviour. Vandalism and crime will
> be major problems and will greatly increase the workloads of police
> probation officers, educationalists and many others. . . .
>   Another tragic aspect of the situation is that youths are being taught
> to hate those of a different religion, and another generation of bigots
> will be appearing on the Northern Irish scene.

Pace describes itself as the journal where Protestant and
Catholic encounter in peace, and is produced by the organisation of the
same name: Protestant and Catholic Encounter. To a meeting of the
local branch my hostess and myself are bound.

That meeting is in the technical institute which stands in great style by
the river Strule where the Model School, that was Protestant primary,
used to stand. We, the boys who went to the Irish Christian Brothers on
Mount St Columba, had one great grudge against Sammy Henderson
and Geordie Mullan and Isaac Hempton and all the boys that went to
the Model: and it was neither political nor sectarian. In that Town we
did, and still do, go easy on the likes of that. No, the Model was
coeducational and the Brothers, notoriously, was not: no investigative
or experimental facilities were provided during class or between classes.
The Loreto convent school was far away on the other side of the Hill
and the parochial house, with three priests in it, stood between. So
Sammy and Geordie and Isaac, who was later to die a hero at the hands
of the Japanese, could tell us all the fancy tales in the world and we
could only hope that they were telling us lies, but fear in sour envy that
they might be telling the truth.
Ah well, the thoughts of youth are long long thoughts.
Between the old Model and the Strule water stood some very tall
trees: and it occasionally came to pass that, round and about Easter,
tricoloured flags of the Irish Republic would sprout from the tops of
those trees which were, of course, as British as Sherwood Forest: and
the tree-trunks might sweat sticky tar and become scabbed with barbed-
wire so that no man of the Royal Ulster Constabulary who valued his

uniform would or could climb up to take the treasonable flags down. The only man to profit by this seasonal operation was a sort of retired steeplejack who, for a small sum, would defy tar and barbed wire and altitude, and the gates of hell. He was undeterred by any Republican principles and unaffected by any other, and once he asked me to thank one of the flag-planters for helping him to make a few extra shillings around Easter: he was aware that that flag-planter was my brother.

Dear God, but it was an innocent sort of world.

And in we go to the meeting where Protestant and Catholic encounter. The lecture-theatre fills up. The names, headed by Scott and Murnaghan, Bell and Mulhern, Wilson and O'Reilly, speak for themselves. There are two Loreto nuns, and the rector of St Columba's and his wife, and a Maxwell and a Coll and McCrory and many others. Elizabeth Maxwell, from the editorial of *Pace* in Belfast talks most instructively about her experiences on organisations that have in many places worked for peace and reconciliation: and particularly in postwar Europe. It has been a strenuous yet, I'd say, a rewarding life, and she speaks about it with clarity and modesty. Above all, she talks with eloquence about the problems of the young who have not known peace as a background to their growing-up. This local branch of *Pace* has encouraged the young people in the schools to put down in poems their thoughts on the necessity for peace, and the results are most interesting:

One young, under-fifteen, poet says with sound sense:

> We are making no one happy
> With the war, this present day
> There'll be no one left for freedom
> If we carry on this way.

Another, with a Swiftian sourness, wonders if peace can be found anywhere in anyone, in soldiers with guns or in priests with prayer-books: peace is in the heart and mind. Another wonders that the world should be full of people whose only friends seem to be bombs and bullets and guns. Another says: 'I was only three or four when the peace stopped. I don't really remember anything before the troubles.' And another:

Sometimes there's peace
And sometimes there's trouble,
And after it all
There's nothing but rubble.

And in another prize-winning poem the poet has enemy speaking to
enemy. An odd faint echo here of Wilfrid Owen:

And then he said:
When this is past,
For it cannot last,
When all this blood is shed,
Will you turn round and shake my hand
And I'll hold up my head.

Poems cannot, God knows, create peace: or, perhaps, God does
know that they might or might help to. But these poems seem to me to
be much preferable, in these times, to war songs or patriotic ballads.
For one of the evil effects of present horrors is that a man may feel guilty
about singing even in privacy and while shaving, some of the songs his
mother sang. The Provos and/or the conditions that have produced
them have polluted even the old songs.

Having no poems to offer to the gathering I read a story.

Round and round the Town I go on the morning after the meeting. A
niece most obligingly does the driving. Never have I seen the Town
look so well, nor the people in it more happy. That's saying a lot in the
times that are in it. The sun is shining, I'll admit, and the blossoms, as
I've said, are out in high style, but the place is spotless, not a scrap of
dirty paper to be seen, and to anyone coming nowadays from Dublin
that's by way of a bonus and a surprise.

Only sixteen thousand people, I'll also admit, and Dublin has the
most of a million. A dirty million, a taximan said to me one day, and he
was a real Dublinman and not an import like myself. He was being
harsh and unfair to a lot of people. Yet in Donnybrook, Dublin, I live
beside a bustop, and the things that come in from the bus-queue and
over the garden hedge would astound you. Even: one day after a rugby
match up the road I found three fine young men from one of our best
schools urinating behind the hedge. They had just come out of the

boozer where, to repeat the hoary old gibe, they had been deterred by seeing the word 'Gentlemen' written on a door. But I'm not now in Dublin nor Donnybrook, and round and round I go, round and round the Town I was reared in. The new estates on the fringe are well-planned and beautifully kept. There's a fine one at Strathroy where on wide and windy acres, where the Fairywater meeets the Strule, I saw my first coursing-match and my first aeroplanes ascending and descending like the angels on Jacob's ladder. Somebody's flying circus. Away back about the time of Lindbergh.

In my time (say the Thirties), there were five or six thousand people here, not counting the soldiers in the barracks. That was how we then expressed it but it may well be that the expression has fallen into disuse. For the barracks is not any more, as it then was, a part of the Town: and some of my best days were spent idling around it, around the stables where the officers still kept a few horses, or watching the display on the parade ground, or wandering the wide acres of the halfmoon holm and along the great curve of the Strule that gave the holm its shape, or playing football for Omagh Corinthians (we grandly called ourselves) against tough teams of young soldiers, or even suffering somewhat in the gymnasium where, by a special arrangement between the Barracks and the Brothers, we were put through our paces or put through paces arbitrarily chosen for us by Corporal Wheeler and Sergeant Mitchell and Sergeant-Major Weir. That last-named gave us our first chance of studying the accent of a genuine son of London.

Nowadays the soldiers walk out only in armed patrols or move in armoured trucks: and because of the destabilisers and creators of the new Ireland there are barriers here and there on the streets. Gates to our town now, a woman says to me.

Round and round and round the Town and up that Cannonhill road about which I've written in a printed book. About and around this Town I seem to have written a lot, lies and truth, and lies and truth mixed. The Cannonhill road is all houses now and has a new name: but this is how it was.

The Cannonhill road went up from the Town in three steps, but those steps could only be taken by Titans. Halfways up the second step or steep hill there was on the right-hand side, and inset into the high hedgerow, a tarred timber barn behind which some of the young as

fancied, and some as didn't, used to box. My elder brother there
chopped one of the Town's bullies, who was a head-fighter, on the soft
section of the crown of his head as he came in charging like a bull, and
that cured him of head-fighting for a long time. Every boy should have
an elder brother who can box.

That barn belonged to that farmer (he has been already mentioned),
who would leave a team of horses standing in a field and go follow a
brass band for the length of the day. Since the Town, as we have been
told, had two brass bands, one military and one civilian, his sowing was
always dilatory and his harvests very close to Christmas. He also owned
a butcher-shop in the Town and he had the word Butcher painted out
and replaced by the word Flesher, which some joker had told him was
more modern and polite but which a lot of people thought wasn't
exactly decent.

If you looked back from Cannonhill, the prospect, or perhaps it
should be the retrospect, was really something: the whole Town, spires
and all, you could even see clear down into some of the streets: the
winding river or rivers, the red brick of the county hospital, already
mentioned, as also Arethusa Glenhordial of the pure mountain springs,
and Gortin Gap and Mullagharn and the tips of Sawel and Dart in the
high Sperrins.

Sometime in the past, nobody knew when, there must or may have
been a gun-emplacement on Cannonhill so as to give the place its
name. Some of the local learned men talked vaguely about Oliver
Cromwell, but he was never next or near the place. There were,
though, guns there in 1941 when a visit from the Germans seemed
imminent and, indeed, they came near enough to bomb Belfast, and
Pennyburn in Derry City, and were heard in the darkness over our
Town, and the entire population of Gallows Hill took off for refuge up
the three titanic steps of the Cannonhill road. It was a lovely June night,
though, and everybody enjoyed themselves . . .

That's from the story I read to that meeting on the banks of the Strule,
and more to follow:

If any one of those merry refugees had raced on beyond the ridge of
Cannonhill they would have found themselves, Germans or no
Germans, in the heart of quietness. The road goes down in easy curves
through good farmland to the Drumragh river and the old graveyard
where the gateway was closed with concrete and stone long before my

time and the dead sealed off forever. There's a sort of stile made out of protruding stones in the high wall and within: only age and desolation, a fragment of an oratory wall that might be medieval, waist-high stagnant grass, table tombstones long made anonymous by weather and moss and lichen, a sinister hollow like a huge shellhole in the centre of the place where the dead, also anonymous, of the great famine of the 1840s were thrown coffinless, one on top of the other. A man who went to school with me used to call that hollow the navel of nothing and to explain in gruesome detail why and how the earth that once had been mounded had sunk into a hollow.

That same man ran away from home in 1938 to join the British Navy. He survived the sinking of three destroyers on which he was a crew-member: once, off the Faroes; once, for a change of temperature, in the Red Sea; and a third time at the battle of Crete. It may be possible that the crew of the fourth destroyer he joined looked at him with some misgiving. A fellow Townsman who had the misfortune to be in Crete as a groundsman with the RAF when the Germans were coming in low and dropping all sorts of unpleasant things to the great danger of life and limb, found a hole in the ground where he could rest unseen, and doing no harm to anybody, until he caught the next boat to Alexandria.

When he crawled into the hole who should be there but the thrice-torpedoed sailor reading the *Ulster Herald*? He said hello and went on reading. He was a cool one, and what I remember most about him is the infinite patience with which he helped me when, impelled by a passion for history, I decided to clean all the table-tombstones in old Drumragh and recall from namelessness and oblivion the decent people who were buried there. It was a big project. Not surprisingly it was never completed, never even properly commenced, but it brought us one discovery: that one of the four people, all priests, buried under a stone that was flat to the ground and circled by giant yews was a MacCathmhaoil, (you might English it as MacCarvill), who had in local history been known as the Sagart Costarnocht because he went about without boots or socks and who in the penal days of proscribed Catholicism had said Mass in the open air at the Mass-rock on Corraduine mountain.

For that discovery our own parish priest, that renowned Dr John McShane, praised us from the pulpit. He was a stern Irish Republican, before that description had been sadly befouled, who had been to the

Irish college in Rome, had met D'Annunzio and approved of him and who always spoke of the six counties of northeast Ulster as *Hibernia Irredenta*. As I have already mentioned. He was also an antiquarian, and in honour of the past and the shadow of the proscribed bare-footed priest, he had read the Mass one Sunday at the rock on Corraduine and watched, in glory on the summit like the Lord himself, as the congregation trooped in over the mountain from seven separate parishes.

This ground is littered with things, cluttered with memories and multiple associations . . .

When I told that story I called it, 'The Night We Rode With Sarsfield', but it had little to do with Patrick Sarsfield, Earl of Lucan, gallant captain of horsemen. Some slight liberties with the truth I may have taken in the passage I there quoted or echoed or something. My father told me never to spoil a good story for the sake of the truth. Henry James, more elaborately, said that the art of fiction lay not in telling what had happened but what should have happened. But that story about my dear dead friend, Michael Mossey, and his three destroyers and his visit to the ancient island of Crete, is no lie: and is attested to by his and my fellow-Townsman, Brian McGale.

Ah Michael, long gone, the miles we walked and cycled together, the hours we spent on the banks of the Drumragh with rod and line, or on the waters of Lough Muck, Loch na Muice, the lake of the mythical pig of Celtic legend who left his mark and his name all over Ireland, the island whose shape was changed by enchantment into the likeness of a monstrous black pig floating on the ocean to baffle and bewilder the wandering Milesians. Who could have thought, Michael, that you would have survived, on the water, perils that would have halted more than the Milesians?

Here at this bridge by the old graveyard of Drumragh we are happy one June evening torturing two unfortunate frogs in the hope of tempting a pike apiece. We feel we are observed. We look up. Over the parapet the heads of two Christian Brothers, one stout and gentle, one stout and cross.

'Splendid, splendid,' says the stout and gentle. 'Our disciples of Izaak.'

'Splendid, splendid,' says the stout and cross. 'Make up on the riverbank what you miss in the classroom.'

Meant not for Michael but for me who had just distinguished myself by some scholastic catastrophe or other.

But, Michael, you looked them calmly in the eyes on my behalf. We nicknamed you the Dead Man because you could wear, when it suited, the moveless gaze and face-muscles of Buster Keaton.

'Books,' you said, ' 'tis a dull and endless strife.'

And added with the composure of the man who wrote it: 'Come hear the woodland linnet. He sings more sweet, and 'pon my life there's more of wisdom in it.'

So they went their decent way, both laughing, and left us to the June peace of the river.

It's a long long way from Crete to that old grey humped bridge and the grave of the barefooted priest.

We are at lunch in a fine stone house five or six miles southwest of the Town. The hostess says: 'There may have been no integration in the schools. But there was integration on the way home from school. Oh, all very modest and innocent. We all met about the Station Brae, Catholics and Protestants, boys and girls, and cycled home together.'

With some sadness she mentions the names of two men who went to school with me, both now dead. One: a school-teacher all his life who had just built himself a fine house for his retirement, and then died, not so long ago, on the eve of that retirement. The other: a strange, brilliant man who was senior to me in my schooldays, a fine scholar whom, being a bit of an oddity myself, I much admired. He was a fine footballer too. His life had ranged from school-teaching in time of peace to the RAF in wartime: and he died, perhaps after a long melancholy, never quite finding the world he was searching for.

With those two young men, and with many others all young and laughing, the lady of the house had, when she was a young girl, cycled the happy road home by the canyon (the only word), and the corkscrew corners at the Flush, by Fireagh Orange Hall and over the Creevan burn at Cavanacaw schoolhouse and through the woods of Clanabogan where lived Felix Kearney, the balladman who wrote 'The Hills Above Drumquin'. She had known Felix well, as had my mother who came from Drumquin:

I have seen the Scottish Highlands, they have beauties rare and grand.
I have journeyed in the Lowlands, 'tis a cold and heartless land.
But I often toiled content, for when each hard day's work was done
My heart went back at sunset to the hills above Drumquin.

The corkscrew corners at the Flush have been straightened by a motor-road. The Flush flows underground. On the journey out from the Town I could see neither the Orange hall nor the Creevan burn. Yet I knew that over the fence my own country was still there, and Pigeon Top mountain, with its mass-rock at Corraduine, was plain to be seen.

'A little out of the Town,' the lady says, 'there was a railwayman's white cottage, just room for it between the road and the railway. We used to stop at the gate there, all of us, from the Loreto convent and the Brothers and the Protestant Academy, and cheer our friends as they passed out by train for Fintona and Dromore and Trillick and Ederney and Irvinestown. All day long we had been with them at school but it was part of the day's ritual to stand at the gate and cheer.'

The six of us, and one of us is a Scots lady, around the luncheon table agree that what the scholars in school-buses, boys and girls all in together, nowadays may gain in rough and tumble they may lose in fresh air, healthy exercise and knowledge of the countryside. Séamus Heaney, the poet, I suggest, from his memories of schooldays on the shore of Lough Neagh and from his affection for a poem by John Clare, would also agree. The idea pleases all of us in this house of stone and fine carved wood, sunny gardens all around it: and even though the woods of Clanabogan, like the woods of Kilcash, are down, the surrounding fields are well cared for and content. This perhaps is the peace the children were writing about and the people desiring.

'One morning in Greenock,' the Scots lady says, 'I heard you on the radio talking about Clanabogan.'

Talking, indeed, I had been about an auction held hereabouts in the year of the battle of Dunkirk. The late Rev. Mr Gumley wasn't it, his books and some other effects being auctioned in the old rectory? With Laurence Loughran, a friend since 1931, I cycled out from the Town to the auction: Laurence, then a young teacher with a job and pay and all; myself, home out of hospital and without a job or a penny or a prospect in the world, and very happy just to be home again. The pennies *pro tempore* were liberally supplied by that elder brother and, anyway, at that time one didn't seem to need much more than books and good companions.

The crocuses were out in bravery and glory on the lawn around the rectory. Out of a few lots of books that Larry bought he gave me my choice. There was the Globe Spenser and a beautiful George Herbert with engravings over which Mr Gumley must often have lovingly lingered. The Spenser has travelled to two good friends in San Francisco. The Herbert I have passed on to the next generation.

Back in the Town we watched a young man called Butler, who was married into the Allens, a Protestant family of handsome girls who lived across the road from the house I was reared in, ride up and down that road on the finest autocycle we had ever seen. We envied him. He was killed that summer in France.

No ghosts outside there today in the bright garden. For Dick Bell of Protestant and Catholic Encounter and myself, the lady of the house draws a map of the roads round by Lough Muck. On whose secretive waters I wish once again to gaze. The roads are twisty and the best memory may err.

Next day, from the bus stalled at the traffic lights for a while as I leave the Town I watch three British soldiers on patrol, three young fellows, one bespectacled. They walk in the odd way that soldiers on the peacetime streets of Today walk when they expect to be shot or to shoot. Never thought I'd see that on these streets. Lord God, the things I could tell those young fellows about this Town.

The problems of the young who have not peace as a background to their growing-up?

But here in this Town and on the hills and in the valleys around it, my companions and myself knew peace.

Carefully as I examine the matter I cannot honestly find that to say what I have just said is merely to give way to nostalgia, a longing for the past, before life, as we call it, had come along with a lot of questions that have remained unanswered, or half-answered or poltroonishly ignored. Am I like the village idiot mentioned in the Abbey Theatre play by Louis D'Alton? If food were offered to him when he was hungry he would try to give it away because he was kind-hearted and he thought everybody else was the way he was: like hungry. But if he were full, replete, satiate, stuffed to the gorge and if food were offered to him he

would do his damnedest to get it down because he thought that
everybody else was stuffed to the gorge etc., and wouldn't thank him for
the gift. Because I was happy here and then, do I now imagine that
everybody else in this place and at that time was also happy? Was the
happiness due to my disposition? Or to my people? Or luck or accident
or the whim of the gods or the temporary neglectfulness of what
Herman Melville's Ishmael called: 'That intangible malignity which
has been from the beginning: to whose dominion even the modern
Christians ascribe one-half of the worlds: which the ancient Ophites of
the east worshipped in their Statue devil . . .'

   Round and round this Town I'll go, walking back into the years
between 1929, say, and 1940, searching for answers, not hoping much
to find them but, at any rate, luxuriating in the memory of the place, or
places, as it then was, or they then were.

SIX

The Gold Ring

Labour for learning before you grow old,
For learning is better than silver or gold:
Silver and gold they may vanish away,
But learning, proud learning will never decay:
And a man without learning, wearing good clothes,
Is like a gold ring in a pig's nose . . .

An odd ambiguity there in the old rural jingle. Does the gold ring stand for the good clothes or the learning?

Anyway, 'twill serve as an introduction to my study of my education.

One day in the 1970s in Donnybrook in Dublin, a man said to me that in fifty years the nuns had altered out of all knowing.

'Look at that young one now,' he said, 'sprinting for a bus.'

Fair enough, on the far side of Morehampton Road a young woman of the conventual variety was legging it along in fine style to catch a number ten to get out to the campus at Belfield for her university studies. The great St Teresa of Avila said that haste was the enemy of devotion, but then the great St Teresa of Avila never had to catch a bus to Belfield.

'And would you care to hear what I saw last Sunday,' the man said. 'Two of them coming out of a shop reading an English Sunday newspaper: and I remember the time when the priests used to preach against the English Sunday newspapers: and only last month there was a picture in the paper here that was an unholy show: two nuns at some class of a broadcasting conference in the Royal Dublin Society in Ballsbridge, one of them in a tweed suit and a short skirt and the other in trousers. A nun in trousers.'

To attempt to console the good man I reminded him that one of those nuns had been American and the other from the Philippines, and it might very well be that they knew no better in those places. But, unconsoled, he left me and went on his way muttering, reminding me of one of those odd characters who used to spring to brief, enigmatic life in the meditations of Myles na Copaleen. Didn't one of his people once say in a tone of apocalyptic warning: 'There's nothing but trousers in Russia.'

Yet that melancholy, disapproving man left me thinking his basic theory was sound enough: in fifty years the nuns have altered out of all knowing, at any rate in outward appearance: and it is now sixty-six years since I met my first nun, two nuns to be exact, and you can take my bible oath on it that neither of them was wearing trousers. There was Sister Patrick. There was Sister Kevin: that wasn't her real name, it wasn't even her real name in religion, but it is possible that in this world or the next she may be around somewhere and I'm taking no chances. Sister Patrick was fat and smiling and quite incapable of harm. Sister Kevin was one tough cookie.

At the time of my first encounter with her I had just passed my third birthday. You may be inclined to question the reliability of my observation at that time, and of my memory here and now. But there are certain things that stay in the memory for ever. The desks that we sat at or in, I can see them still. The work, if that's what you would call it, that we were supposed to do. The handkerchiefs attached by safety-pins to our jerseys, the jerseys of the boys, that is, for we were co-educational. Nor, since nobody had ever heard of Freud, was our contiguity regarded as any risk to holy purity, or anything else. The handkerchiefs, so pinned on to us, were, quite literally, to hand for use and we could not easily lose them. The girls kept their handkerchiefs up their sleeves on elastic bands, nor could we ever find out how that one worked.

But the wells on my path to learning in that harem of a school were poisoned by the affair of the schoolreader and by the blow Sister Kevin caught me on the knuckles with her cane when I was absorbed in drawing funny faces with spittle and fingertip on the glossy, brown wooden desk.

'Wipe the desk clean this instant,' she said. 'You naughty little boy.'

You can see the reasons I had for loving Sister Kevin. She and that cane were famous. They were even in the Pancake Tuesday rhyme:

> Pancake Tuesday's a very happy day.
> If we don't get our holidays we'll all run away.
> Where will we run to? Up Fountain Lane,
> When we see Sister Kevin coming with the cane.

I have, often since, wondered what she had against men. But I bested her over the business of the schoolreader. This is what happened. It was a lovely schoolreader: sixteen pages of simple sentences, big print, coloured pictures. It told the most entrancing stories. This one, for instance: 'My dog, Rags, has a house. He has a little house of his own. See, his name is over the door.'

Or this: 'Mum has made buns for tea. She has made nice hot buns.'

Or yet another: 'When the children went to the zoo they liked the elephant best of all. Here is the elephant with happy children on his back.'

That elephant I was contemplating with sombre and scientific interest when Sister Kevin put her hand on my schoolreader and said: 'Your sister tells me you have one of these at home.'

Which was true enough. But to have one copy, which my mother had bought me, at home and to have another copy, supplied by regulations, in school, gave that miracle of coloured picture and succinct narrative the added wonder of twins and two elephants, or of having two of anything. So when Sister Kevin, soaring to the top of her flight in the realms of wit, said that one reader should be enough for such a little boy, and all the female mixed-infants giggled, I saw red and grabbed: leaving Sister Kevin speechless with shock and turning over and over in her hand a leaf that said on one side: ' "Here comes the aeroplane," said Tom.' And on the other side: 'When the children came home from town they had much to tell Mum.'

Gripping the rest of the reader I glared at the nun who was white in the face with something, fright or fury, at this abrupt confrontation with the male forces of violence and evil. She looked at me long and thoughtfully. Fortunately for me she was that day perambulating without benefit of cane. She said: 'Naughty boy. Now your poor mother will have to pay for the book you destroyed. Stand in the corner under the clock with your face to the wall until hometime.'

Which I did, tearless, my face feverish with victory, because that onset with Sister Kevin had taught me things about women that some men never find out. And, staring at the brown varnished wainscotting in the corner of the room, I made my resolve: As long as I'd live I'd never go back to that schoolful of women. I would go to the Brothers with the big boys. And I knew that my mother would create no obstacles because if I could defy Sister Kevin and live, I was more than a match for my mother. It was, I had found out, a man's world . . .

Today, I'm not so sure. And I wonder would my world have been different if Sister Kevin had been wearing tartan slacks. There's no holy rule that says that a dainty morsel in slacks could not also be a terror with the cane on Pancake Tuesday or any other day.

At any rate I kept my vow and crossed over to the Christian Brothers and the big boys: and my first Christian Brother was a man called Lynch, brother in the flesh to General Liam Lynch of tragic memory: and when I read Major Florry O'Donoghue's life of Liam Lynch I found out that the first teacher the Lynch boys ever had was a man with the same name as myself and down in the southerly part of the country where the Kielys or Kileys or Keilys or Na Cadhlaigh or Na Cadhla come from: a harmless coincidence meaning nothing in particular yet one of those things that give a subtle, perhaps a magic quality to the business of living.

Thus my brief affair with the holy sisters of Loreto came to an abrupt end. Somewhere in the family archives there may be a portrait from that period. Such portraits came in inch-wide strips and six at a time. It shows, or showed, a pudgy, sullen three-year-old with untidy hair, and that handkerchief pinned to the gansey: a disgrace, I'd say, and a reproach to an elder sister, for elder sisters did not wish to be incommoded at school by little brothers or, if they were compelled to bear them company, then they treated them to a pretty sharp discipline: and the task of convoying me to the holy house of Loreto, which had once been convoyed over land and sea by angels, was given to a neighbour's daughter, May Kavanagh. May was no believer in that business about a straight line being the shortest distance between two points and to her I owe an early and sound knowledge of the geography of my hometown. Had I lived longer in her company I might have rivalled Henry the Navigator: but literature and the pictorial arts swept us apart.

The Brothers I had studied at an angle from a sitting or kneeling, sometimes standing for the gospel, position in the side aisle dedicated to the mother of God. They entered through the doorway from a passage, that led into the sacristy, they crossed to the nave, took their places in the first pew on the gospel side and right under the pulpit. Six of them. They changed over the years from 1923 onwards until I left the Town in 1937, not left totally, never totally: anyway the Town followed me.

There were three priests: the then parish priest, Fr Phil O'Doherty, old and silvery and slow as a coachhorse; Fr Lagan, tall, grave, gentlemanly but formidable, brother to a great Chestertonian girth of a medical man, Dr Barney Lagan; then a Fr McFaul, succeeded by a McGilligan, and others and others. Three priests and six brothers.

The story about Fr Lagan was that once on the Twelfth of July, the feast of King William, Fr Lagan was standing at the church gate, the limping spires soaring away above him. The music and drumming of the Orange bands was far away in the distance. The conflux of Castle Street, George's Street and Church Street was quiet and sunny, and down along Church Street came two drunk and wandering Orangemen, one young, one old. So the young one surveyed Fr Lagan, in all his Roman regimentals, and said: 'To hell with the Pope.'

On which the old one struck the young one and knocked him down and the priest said: 'Well, he was rude, I'll admit, but perhaps you were a bit rough on him.'

And the old one said: 'The ill-mannered wee nur. He took the words outa me mouth.'

Six Irish Christian Brothers in one pew before the high altar of the Sacred Heart: Brother Keane, the superior, a small bespectacled man, four others who are now only shadowy dark shapes, a sixth, also small, a dreaming gentle face, rimless spectacles which may have been a rarity at that time and in that place. Their delicate glistening may have caught my attention. The Wee Brother who wore them was a demigod with shining eyes, or, as A.E. said about the druidess, seeing with subtle eyes

the shining light. He commanded my devotion: so that when, as a
refugee from Loreto, I was led by my mother up the slope of what was
called Mount St Columba to the door of the big oblong stone building
to ask specially, since I was under age, for admission I refused to entrust
myself to anyone but the Wee Brother. Even the good-natured Brother
Superior, small as he was, did not meet my specifications. So Brother
Lynch was sent for and recognised.

Each one of the long school-benches then in use would have
accommodated about a dozen young men, age of four and upwards
with the exception of myself who had been admitted under age, as I
said. One of those benches was much involved in the only notable
event that I recall from those earliest days of my educational career: that
event had to do with religion.

  Big Billy, Big Andy, Big John, all big for their age and their age was
older than anybody else because they were a bit slow on the uptake
academically and should have been two grades or so further on towards
the Pierian spring or whatever. It was customary at the end of the day for
the class to kneel on the seating part of the benches and follow the Wee
Brother in a singsong recital of the litany of the Blessed Virgin: 'Ark of
the Covenant pray for us, House of God pray for us, Tower of Ivory pray
for us.' Because of their size and weight Big Billy, Big Andy and Big
John were allowed or commanded to stand, not kneel up. But one day,
in a general fit of absentmindedness, they knelt up and the bench
collapsed. Never since have I taken part in the litany nor thought for a
moment of those strange celestial titles, or symbols, without hearing
again that crash and splintering, and seeing Big Billy, Big Andy and Big
John down among the rubble.

  Big Andy had close-cropped, curly hair, was short-sighted, wore
thick-lensed spectacles, was gentle, if morose and, as far as I remember,
distinguished himself only by one action in his life. One day a young
lady well-known to both the Inniskillings and the Royal Irish Fusiliers,
and with the quite classical name of Lucy Wordsworth, upset his
bicycle which was poised on one pedal at the kerb. As she stooped
politely and penitently to pick it up he administered to her an
unmerciful kick up the backside. But no: some years later when we were
in fourth class under Brother Doyle and, after him, Brother Walker,
Big Andy had a murderous battle with Big John: in and out from the

classroom to the narrow yard that divided the secondary and the primary, a battle titanic and indecisive and a terrifying spectacle for smaller boys. After which, they became and remained good friends.

By fourth class (1928–9), Big John had developed a hairstyle, simple but effective, brilliantine lavishly applied to black hair which was then combed, brushed and manually plastered straight back until it shone to the sun like a priceless carapace. He was always half-an-hour late in the morning and it was a most exciting experience for the entire class to see through the glass panel in the upper half of the door the hands of Big John smoothing down that shimmering shell, preparing a face to meet the faces he would meet. He had more important things on his mind than fourth-class scholarship: for he was one of the first men in my world who was really into motorbikes, not the expensive models that young people possess nowadays but machines that he made himself out of fragments collected here and there, even from that smouldering Garden of Eden, the Town-dump, where all sorts of curios and antiquities could be unearthed or unashed.

He and his people lived on Church Hill, a steep medieval thoroughfare with tessellated sidewalks where it was not then unusual to toss the dishwater, nothing worse, into the gutter or vennel: and where once, in a dreaming mood, I was abruptly awakened by John's mother giving me, quite by accident, the contents of the wash-basin. But most apologetically she dried me and fed me on sweetmeats until, like Kitty of Coleraine, I would for that pleasure have been drenched all over again.

From the small yard behind the house the roars of Big John's developing monsters arose to be heard for great distances, roaring, revving, backfiring until the moment of revelation was at hand and, under his sable shining brillantined helmet the knight rode forth. The neighbours never complained. Great things were happening. Lindbergh was up there somewhere. A new world was on the way.

Where did he ride to when those days were over? To Britain when Hitler was battering at the gates? Coventry perhaps: it had a great name for bicycles.

Big Billy was an innocent sort of fellow, gentle in his ways but so strong that not even the hardiest would go out of their way to pick a fight with him. With his fists he was as skilful as he was strong and he grew up to be a reputable boxer, acquiring, on the path of glory, another name. That has happened if not quite in the same way, to many people: Molotov, Hitler, Saki, Fiona MacLeod, George Orwell, Voltaire, Cassius Clay, Mark Twain and others. Matched in a bout in the barracks, and when he was still but a novice, against a pretty tough Fusilier Kluterbuck from Yorkshire or somewheres east, Billy, whether by accident or design or agonised despair, struck the fusilier a severe blow in a place, like the Dardanelles, where no gentleman normally strikes another. The resultant roars of Kluterbuck were heard beyond the Strule and as far away as the rural glades of Killyclogher where, by the crystal burn, the lovely girls walked singing: and forever after Billy was known by the name of his stricken foe which, for extra force and punch, alliterated with his own surname.

But in his early academic career Big Billy used his strength and skill only to succour weaklings and to frustrate bullies, and myself and many another were in his debt for a protected peace in which to pursue our studies. Last time I heard or saw him was at a wake in a house in old Castle Street. 1935 or 1936? Who the corpse was I cannot remember. The snuff and the clay pipes and porter still went round: and what I do remember and can see quite clearly is the copy of some London illustrated magazine that Mark Meehan was displaying to the savants in one corner of the kitchen. The corpse was away upstairs in a quiet room with only prayers and tears and flowers and candles.

There was an article in that magazine saying ominously that Germany still had an army, pictures in sepia of helmeted men crouching by guns.

Mark Meehan was a wise guy. He read all the available magazines and all the newspapers. He was much admired by his mother. He wore a good, brown, belted overcoat and a flat cloth-cap, or duncher as they used to call it in Belfast, with a button on the top of it: and a classy, silk scarf. He told us all about a man he called Hilther and about all the great things that Hilther was doing for the German people. At regular intervals Billy, overpowered both by Mark's erudition and the exploits of Hilther, would say: 'Jasus, he's not chuman.'

That description followed me all through the war years and for a long time afterwards when the darkest secrets were emerging like monsters from the camps: Jasus, he's not chuman.

*

Those then were the three wise men who stood by the postern when I rode out on the quest for learning: although, strictly speaking, the Brothers and Big Jim Gunn had more to do with my education, and later on Michael J. Curry and Leo Sullivan and Anthony Shannon and Frank McLaughlin.

Brother Hamill has been with us already, calmly dusting his hands as the train thundered down on him on the echoing metal of the Linn Bridge: with his Chinese experience behind him and his brotherhood in the flesh with Mickey Hamill, the great centrehalf. Which meant that in a town then much devoted to soccer football he was a learned and professional adviser on all matters connected with the round ball: three or four teams in the Town and two or three among the soldiers. There he still stands on the sideline, a cloud of pipesmoke rising above him and drifting off in the prevailing wind towards his native Belfast. He is exhorting, with the assistance of an occasional rallentando of rough language, the young men who are the best the Town possesses: 'Keep it on the carpet, Hog! Steady, John, now . . . Shoot! Style, Mathew, style, you're a credit to all before you and connected with you.'

Mathew Doherty and John Gormley became noted professional footballers. A Dublin taxidriver who, in the course of driving me somewhere in 1983, discovered that I came from that Town said that one famous man came from there and his name was Mathew Doherty.

Brother Burke and Brother Burke, one stout and robust and known as Busty, a Dublinman and an old boy of Blackrock College, in that City, and who, on that account, set us all playing rugby football against the Protestant schools and earned thus the enmity of the Town's true Gaels, among whom there was then surfacing St Enda's Gaelic Football Club, called so grandly after the school Patrick Pearse had kept in Dublin, and rode his wingéd horse.

If people cannot agree on how to kick a football it will be hard to get them to agree about anything else.

The second Burke, inevitably but most inaptly nicknamed Lanky, was tall, darkhaired, handsome, a Tipperary man from Portroe which is high above Lough Derg and the Shannon, and he had the rich easy accent that you will find in that part of the country. It was said of him, and I can see how it might have been true, that every woman in the Town, young and old, was secretly and hopelessly, because of that business of celibacy, in love with him. Like most Tipperary men he knew how to handle a hurling-stick and did his best to teach the more fervent of the true Gaels, including my brother, the nature of the game that went back into our mythologies and, by the aid of which, young Setanta, the son of Sualtim, choked with a ball or sliotar, the hound of Cullan, smith to the high king, Conor, and thus afterwards earned for himself the name of Cuchullain, the hound of Cullan. But if Tyronemen had ever played the game they had well lost the knack by the 1930s, and the last men known to handle sticks in that part of the world might well have been the pikemen that, it was said, the Great O'Neill drilled in Glenlark, in the mountains to the northeast, to face the soldiers of the great Elizabeth. The first of the name.

That day on the bridge by the old graveyard of Drumragh the stout and cross Christian Brother had been, as you might have guessed, Busto or Busty Burke. Later in life he was to tell an almost-contemporary of mine that the chief sorrow of his academic career was that I had ever been a pupil of his. He was provoked into that remark when a novel of mine, *In a Harbour Green*, an innocent tale of adolescence or something, was honoured by the Dublin censorship (the first of three novels of mine to be so honoured) with the laurel-wreath of being in general tendency indecent or obscene. That was in the late 1940s. At that time it was about the only honour paid to Irish writers in their own country: and distributed so lavishly that it was almost a disgrace not to be so honoured. Then George Murnaghan, the great lawyer in the Town or the greatest of the many great lawyers in the county's legal headquarters, and the father of another George Murnaghan, a Dublin judge, explained to innocent old Busto the absurd nature of the Dublin censorship: and in his later years in the retirement home at Baldoyle in North Dublin, Busto accepted me almost as a friend.

Hamill died in that same retirement home, much visited on his deathbed by my friend and contemporary, J. G. Macauley and myself. His only sorrow as death approached was that not one of the retired Brothers-in-Christ who surrounded him had ever heard of keeping the ball on the carpet.

'Croke Park,' he would say sadly. 'That's all they talk about or listen to on the radio. Gaelic football. Hurling. Kick a ball or puck a sliotar, as they call it, halfways to the moon. Or as the song says, my goal-ball I'd strike to the lightning of heaven. Then stand around in rings wondering will it ever come down again. The Poc Fada or the Long Puck. What goes up must come down. Any child in primer could tell them that.'

Far far away were the thronging millions of China and the awesome wideness of the Yangtse-kiang flowing forever through his memories. Far far away were the red-and-white jerseys of the Omagh Rovers, and Gormley and Doherty and Hog Kearney and the green grass of the Showgrounds and the Soldiers' Holm and the serpentine Strule flowing between, and far away the town in which he said he had been more at home even than in his native Belfast: and New Drumragh where it was his dying wish to be buried. For some sad reason or other the religious rule was dead set against that, which was a pity, because the whole Town, Protestant and Catholic, would have welcomed him back and walked behind his coffin: as the whole Town had mourned when, in the closing years of his religious life, that same holy rule had cold-bloodedly transferred him elsewhere. He might as well, the people said, have been in the army.

And the stout and gentle brother on the bridge that day was affectionately known to us as Baldy Walker. He was a veteran and had taught in that school in the days of the fathers of some of us, and then been religiously moved somewhere else and then religiously moved back again: to resurface before class one morning in fourth class and be beaming down, with all the kindness of his heart and the radiance of his genuinely bald head, on Snifter Hannigan and myself. We are zealously copying a piece of staff-notation from the master-work produced by a fellow-student who knows a lot more about music than we do.

Our labour of monastic scrivenry is intended, with a few cacophanies deliberately and judiciously inserted, to get us alive through Hamill's music-class. For Hamill knows music from Kreisler to Galli-Curchi and, for a merciful relief, to Harry Lauder, and has school-concerts at which he plays twelve-inch classical recordings, and trains a school-choir to sing at concerts in the Townhall, and that plainchant choir to sing at Feis Doire Cholmcille, and to get second prize. A Derry choir always had to get first. Derry people were notoriously musical.

To both of those choirs, the one for the Townhall and the one for the Derry Guildhall I, in my days as a boy-soprano, belonged: and sang Firsts and whistled Seconds, a phenomenon Hamill stumbled on, by God, in the course of the rendering (that is the exact word) of 'The

Whistling Farmer's Boy' in which you sang the verses, such as they were, and whistled the chorus. So, singing Firsts and whistling Seconds I managed to put the whole First Battalion out of tune.

But on Snifter and myself the sun of innocence shone down.

'It warms my heart,' the Brother said, 'to see young men interested in music.'

Snifter sniffed. Not cocaine. He had a nonstop runny nose. He sniftered with relief at finding out that we were not detected. Perhaps also with a little contempt at discovering that any grown-up person could be so easily fooled. He was a quiet unassuming fellow and he lost, as he grew up, both the snifter and the nickname and lived to be killed as a hero at Anzio-beachead.

That year in fourth class we had as a learned text R. M. Ballantyne's *The Dog Crusoe*, which I then thought one of the best books I had ever read but which I have not, alas, read or seen since then, sixty years ago, and Snifter's music belongs out there on the lone prairie with the three brave young fellows and that high moment of mirth when Henri the half-breed ate the concoction of sour berries: and out there, also, Brother Walker stands up smiling behind his desk to display to us his one experiment in physics. Solemnly from a glass jug he fills a half-pint tumbler with water, stooping down like an enchanter to make certain it is filled to the brim. Solemnly, firmly he presses down a square of cardboard on the beaded rim. Solemnly, now you see it now you don't, he raises the tumbler and turns it upside down: and that's how the waters come down at Lodore over his desk and everything on and in it. Never once, no not once, do I remember his one and only venture into the world of science ending in success. As failure followed failure he learned, at the moment of truth to stand further away from his desk so that nothing suffered but the floor.

My memory of the last time I saw him and it is, as all memories of him are, happy, is from a house in which I then lived in North Dublin City: and from that house, if you stood on the roof, you had a clear view, even on a misty day, of the long and level strand of Dollymount on which Stephen Dedalus cried out to his heavenly god when he saw the young woman with skirts kilted up and wading in the salt water.

But that day in the 1940s and for the kindly Brother from the bridge at old Drumragh it was a privilege and joy to open a bottle of fifteen-year-old at which he sipped with moderation and gentlemanly appreciation.

He resisted all challenges to turn the glass upside down. We hadn't a word to say about James Joyce. Yet Joyce, in a comical sort of way, fits in here: which the same I would rise to explain by climbing up again to the roof of that house in North Dublin City. There below me is the broad seaside road from central Dublin to the Hill of Howth. Beyond that road a narrow run of water where two tides meet and beyond that the dunes and sea-birds and the long strand and the bathers and courting couples and golf-clubs of the Bull Island: which, as we all know, would not be there at all if it had not been for that much maligned man, Captain Bligh of the *Bounty*.

The story is that Bligh, before he moved on to better things, had an admiralty post in Dublin and drew up a plan to protect the port from silting. The plan which included the building of the Bull Wall was put into effect, even if that was not until after Bligh's departure: and the sand that would have blocked the harbour piled up behind the wall and out of the North Bull sandbank, and with the aid of the immortal sea, created the Bull Island. So that had it not been for the Captain, Stephen Dedalus could not have walked on the place to be enraptured by life and the wading sea-bird of a girl.

Nor, without Bligh, could Stephen on his way to that vision have seen the young Irish Christian Brothers pounding in their big rural boots over the planks of the Bull Bridge.

Round about here it would seem to me to have become necessary to make some general statement about the Irish Christian Brothers. As to who and what and why and where from. After all I did spend fifteen to sixteen years of my life more or less under their surveillance. As did many another. When in school and often when round and about the Town.

I have heard them blamed for many things. Like beating education into boys which anyway, and looking at the world the way it now is, does not seem to be such a bad idea. Blamed for the pandy-bat, as it was called in Dublin, or the leather as we called it in the North. But I never found that the Brothers I encountered used it any way but sparingly. And Waterloo was won on the playing-fields of Eton, when and where flogging was all the rage, and there may yet be something to be said for the fraternal pandy-bat.

The Brothers were blamed, also, for teaching to their pupils a sort of die-in-the-ditch Irish patriotism. Not so. But they did teach a sort of national pride and self-respect, and respect for the neighbour. Close my eyes is all I have to do and see Hamill, and two Burkes, one for rugby, one for hurling, both brothers in Christ, men of simple self-sacrifice and, behind them in their Order, a long history of the same.

For instance: Gerald Griffin, the author of *The Collegians*, a most scrupulous man and, because of his soul-racking scruples, the closest to us of any of the Irish novelists of the early nineteenth century, was, it has been said, first drawn to the work of Edmund Ignatius Rice and his followers not so much by their teaching school as by their heroic behaviour among the poor, in Griffin's native Limerick City, during a cholera epidemic. Griffin was later to burn his manuscripts and turn his back on fame and the world, and become a Christian Brother.

There were grim times in Ireland round about June 1816, when the Brothers arrived in Limerick City. Desmond Rushe in his fine biography of Rice has described how the good men set up school in the only place they could find, in Hill's Lane in Irishtown, a 'vast mass of dilapidation, filth and misery'. They even had to beg from door to door to provide decent clothes for the worst-off of their pupils. No wonder the sensitive and austere Gerald Griffin was impressed.

Edmund Rice had been a rich merchant in Waterford City and, when left a widower, he took the words of the Gospel quite literally, and sold what he had and gave to the poor and followed Christ. He had, too, considerable possessions. It seems clear that the death of his wife and the birth of a daughter who was mentally retarded sharpened his perceptions of the nature of the passing vanities of this life. It seems quite as clear that the impulse to give and to deny himself, for the sake of his fellow man, was there from the beginning, was bred into the bone: giving, not with any wild demonstration or public enthusiasm, but with resistless, businesslike, Norman method.

Ireland has had reason to be grateful. Rice thought that the poor, of whom Ireland then had more than her share, needed gainful employment and decent homes, and food and respectable clothes, and books, and education, and the love of God. Books and libraries were very high up on his list. But the love of God, and the unselfish love of his fellow man, ruled over all.

It is a curious thing . . .

Brinsley MacNamara, novelist and early Abbey Theatre playwright who wrote the novel *The Valley of the Squinting Windows*, and a lot more besides, and the privilege of whose freindship I am to have in the Forties and Fifties, prefaced most of his statements with those five words. That was the way he saw the world. He even entitled a collection of his short stories *Some Curious People*. For his autobiography, unfortunately never finished, he picked a title out of Goldsmith: *The Long Vexation*. They were both men from the Irish midlands:

> I still had hopes, the long vexation passed,
> Here to return and die at home at last.

Brinsley could be a rancorous man and was much involved in controversy around the theatre and elsewhere but, since we were of different generations, we had nothing to quarrel about and had also, I flatter myself, a natural compatibility: and there will be much to say about him in the future. For the moment I salute his noble, most impressive Shade, and borrow a phrase.

So, it is a curious thing that the first good apologia for James Joyce that I ever encountered was spoken in class in secondary school by an Irish Christian Brother.

It is also a curious thing that his name was Rice. He was, I think, some sort of a relation of the heroic founder. He came to our Town from the Brothers' school in Newry, County Down, a town that had always enjoyed the reputation of being Gaelic and nationalist and even Republican, God help us, or, as I once heard a decent Dublin girl say: 'Fierce Irish.'

Also: the religious transfer of Brother Rice meant that he replaced Busto Burke who was, as the world would now say, into English rugby while Rice, like Lanko Burke, was very much into Irish hurling and Gaelic football and must, at times, have thought that in his new assignment he was trying to persuade education into the bastards of the Civil Servants of the Raj. Then on top of all that, he encountered Omagh Corinthians. That was a soccor-football team made up of ten of my contemporaries and myself. The English, as we know, invented soccer football, the spinning-jenny, Shakespeare, the Lambeth Walk and the policy of *Divide et Impera*. Although the Romans may have been first at the last-mentioned, as they may have been first at the Lambeth Walk or even at the Highland Fling which, I was once assured

by a drunk man in Newcastle-on-Tyne, was first performed on
Hadrian's Wall. Certainly the English were first with the round ball as a
development from the kicking about of the heads of departed and
decapitated foes: and to a man accustomed to the fierce Irishness of the
boys of Newry, Omagh Corinthians could fairly be regarded as a West
British or colonialist organisation. Fifth columns had not yet been
heard of.

Under our splendid, if imperfectly understood, title we played at
regular intervals with teams from the local Protestant academy and,
across the religious barrier, made friendships with Cathcarts and
Alcorns and Kyles and McFarlanes. Since Alec Hyndman, our right
fullback (whose people were currently Catholic but British-army back
to the time of William of Orange), and myself were also going through
the motions of playing Gaelic football in a streets-league, which had six
teams in the Town, we were solemnly suspended for six months at a
meeting in the Foresters' Hall of the local Gaelic Athletic Association:
for being spotted, by a member of the Gaelic vigilance committee,
playing a foreign game with Protestant boys in a Protestant field. The
religious bit was not mentioned in the formula but it was part of the
meaning.

We played also on the wide and windy acres of the Soldiers' holm
against teams of young soldiers and learned to rough it or, rather, to be
roughed: and to take a beating. Young soldiers thought that an injured
limb meant a few days rest for a young soldier, and had no reason to
think that we could think otherwise: nor that they might not be doing us
a favour by laying us low. They were forthright, decent, young fellows.
One of them in one memorable game was an ex-schoolboy-
international, Scottish, called, I think, Keenan. But Dick Minnis, who
was a big man and a Corinthian and a Canadian, managed to flatten the
Scot: and the balance of justice between nations, teams, and soldiers
and civilians was preserved. Minnis afterwards became a soldier as his
father had been before him.

My own pitiful and insignificant part in those Corinthian exploits
was in a position that was then described as outside-right and may, for
all I know, be still so described. For this I had one qualification: I could
run very fast. But, also, one fatal disqualification: that in the heat of the
conflict I was more likely to run into rather than around the opposing
academic or military defender and, thus, not only to suffer and,

perhaps, cause severe abrasions but, also, to lose possession not only of my wits but of the round ball. Yet I was a devoted Corinthian and, being eloquent, was picked as spokesman to defend our cause when the new Gaelic Brother Superior discovered that, when the eleven of us should have been out on our own Irish field swinging hurls and hitting nothing, we were faraway beyond the serpentine Strule playing soccer with the soldiers of the empire.

He was, Rice, a handsome man with a strong profile and a mane of white hair and he completely shaved away his sidelocks. He listened to me with evident incomprehension. What I was trying to say I do not exactly remember but he sure as God had never heard the like from the embryo Republicans of Iubhar Cinn Tragha, which is Newry or the Yew Tree at the Head of the Strand. He clouted me one on the lug and I had the distinction of being the first and only person he ever struck in that school. He was by no means the violent type: and it may simply have been that my sophistries would have lifted Job from his dunghill. What it all taught me was: Never if you can avoid it, be a spokesman.

And another thing that came between Rice and myself was trigonometry. He elected to teach mathematics. He could have taught anything, as in the course of a few years I found out, but he elected to teach mathematics to a class of dullards in mathematics and, of all the dullards, I was the dullest. Years afterwards, when I had come to know him as a great human being, I dared to ask him if he had done it for a penance and with his eye on the world to come, and he laughed, in a way that may or may not have answered my question.

John Desmond Sheridan, a good humorous writer, once said that at school he suffered a lot from and for trigonometry and then, when he left school, he found out that all the lighthouses were measured. So much did I suffer that if it had not been for R. L. Stevenson's father or grandfather having had something to do with lighthouses I would have loathed the things for the rest of my life. Then one day in the thick of a shower of sines and cosines Rice threw his head back and shook his mane and said: 'James Joyce.' Just the two words and just like that. As if he had seen somebody on the ceiling. We did not know who he was talking to, or about. There was nobody of the name in the class. We looked up and saw nothing and nobody. We were, as I afterwards worked out, about to get the side or fringe benefit of something he had recently read. This was what it was all about.

Somewhere in the South of Ireland, or the Free State, a thundering and puritanical professor had made an attack on the morals of a poet, as evidenced in a new collection of the poet's poems. The poet was F. R. Higgins. Was the collection *The Dark Breed* or *The Gap of Brightness*? I can't recall. The professor roundly condemned passages which he considered lascivious. Lascivious, to us, sounded fine. A definite improvement on sines and cosines. Out of a book Rice read three poems. We listened hopefully but ended up little the wiser. Any evening going home from school through Fountain Lane you could hear better from some of the girls who went with the soldiers. Then in Irish and English he read out more-or-less parallel passages from Douglas Hyde's *The Love Songs of Connacht*. Surely to God nobody could accuse the great scholar Douglas Hyde, who was to become the first president of the Irish Republic, of lasciviousness. So the professor was a fool. Years afterwards I met the man, not in the halls of academia but in connection with a weekly newpaper, and I realised that Rice had been right.

That day, from the defence of Fred Higgins he sailed on to his defence of Joyce, giving us his life and times and literary merit in a splendid speech: as good an introduction to the man as anything I have encountered since. It was the best trigonometry lesson I ever sat through.

After that one disagreement Rice and myself became friends. Books brought us together and the essential goodness of the man which became obvious even to a green and callow youth. When at the Christmas of 1939 I returned to the Town to learn again the business of walking, after a year with the Jesuits, whose fault it wasn't, and eighteen months in an orthopaedic hospital, he was one of the first men to knock on my door. He gave me the run of the Brothers' own private library, a very good one. He gave me for keeps Smith's Latin dictionary, and a Father Dineen with his own name on the flyleaf. I treasure them still.

Then there was Brother Cloke, a Wexfordman, so gentle and quiet that one might easily forget him. Except that round about 1957 he came back into my life on a great day in Binion and Clonmany and Ballyliffin in County Donegal. On that day I watched sheepdog trials on a flat holm by the sea under Binion Head, and drank whiskey and whisky in a tent with tall, tough, crook-bearing men from the Grampians and the Highlands: and found a great house to be put into that novel called *The Captain with the Whiskers*. Without that house, which was revealed to me for the first time on that day, I could never, for good or ill, have written the novel. But I'll come to that *in tempore opportuno*. At the moment it is 1936.

SEVEN

Introibo ad Altare

Two of the many things I never succeeded in becoming were an altar-boy and a Christian Brother.

Although once, and now that I think of it, I was an altar-boy in a sort of temporary capacity when they were calling up the reserves, or the militia, for a special sort of devotion known, with great grandeur, as the Forty Hours Adoration. Mountains of flowers all around the high altar, candles burning for further orders, the shining golden monstrance with the blessed sacrament out of the tabernacle and, as it was said, exposed: and two boys in red soutanes and white surplices on duty as sentries.

And for three years or so of my life, roughly between the ages of twelve and fifteen, I was, rather dubiously, half-enlisted into considering the prospect of becoming a Christian Brother.

There was no reason that I remember why I, in my time, never became an altar-boy. I had nothing against it. Neither had my people. I was the equal, if not the superior, in faith, piety, perseverance and good works to any of my contemporaries: not that that would be saying much. Nor was I too bad at the Latin. There were also certain enviable things about the simple status of being an altar-boy. There were the style and appearance, the surplice and the soutane, and the opportunity for sheer exhibitionism to which the very young are frequently prone. There were the tips at weddings and the sips at the altar-wine, about which latter the uninitiate heard so many, possibly exaggerated, stories. There was also, at least in our parish, a merry party and an excursion to somewhere or other once a year. Against all that there was the danger of being accused of being a cissy: almost as bad as if you had been condemned to music lessons and to being seen in public carrying the telltale violin case.

Never, at any rate, was I to know what it was like from the inside, except on that one occasion when extra manpower was needed to help out with the Forty Hours Adoration. No Latin was required, no movements, no stagecraft. All you had to do was kneel there like a stock or a stone or, as the Americans so delightfully put it, like a bump on a log: and be still as you are beautiful, be silent as the rose, no fidgeting nor crossing of ankles, scratching, nor unnecessary yawning, coughing nor sneezing. The only hazard was the utter boredom. But the veterans, the fulltime professional soldiers, were always decent enough to instruct the raw recruits in the best methods of beating the boredom. You removed the red cover from a simple periodical publication designed by the Jesuits for the edification of the not-overly-literate pious: *The Irish Messenger of the Sacred Heart*. Then you inserted into that cover some more readable material of roughly the same format: and there you were.

The twopenny pamphlets that then dealt with the exploits of the detective Sexton Blake, or with the more open-air exploits of Buffalo Bill, were much favoured. It could be dangerous, as in the army, unless you could trust absolutely the swaddy who was with you on sentry-go. Tales could be told. But generally, the *esprit de corps* was high, and I remember the whole thing as a most rewarding experience: the golden glow of the candles all around, the smell of wax and incense and flowers heavy on the air, and me in the middle of it all and reading about the great adventures of Buffalo Bill.

But, earlier, when I was about six years of age there was one thing about altar-boys that puzzled me very much: the faces were or seemed to be familiar, faces seen in a dream. I had, of course, seen them on the streets of the Town but then, as Thomas Carlyle was later to explain to me, the robes made all the difference: and it took me a long time to realise that the faces were the same faces, the boys the same boys, and that those godlike and arcane creatures did, indeed, walk the earth like mortal men.

My puzzlement was particularly severe in the case of a boy called Francis MacMahon who was created, you might say, to be a sort of perpetual altar-boy: one of those large boys who still wore short trousers when he should long have graduated into longers, who had plump placid white knees, a calm divine face, fair curly hair that was carefully dressed and combed. He died young: and if for a while he intensified, he also finally solved for me that problem of the double identity of altarboys. Sheer hard reasoning convinced me that there could not be two Francis MacMahons. The boy to be seen on the streets of the Town and the boy-god in the red-and-white robes had to be the same person.

Yet there was something else about him that puzzled me. His adoring relatives called him not Francis but Frantie. Now, in my mother's repertoire of songs and ballads there was an odd piece of Victoriana called, 'The Drunkard's Dream'. It told how some poor chap, known to be a ferocious boozer, is seen one day walking about quite sober. So a good superior sort of lady says to him:

> I never see you drunk about,
> Pray, tell what this may mean.

And he answers:

> I had a dream, a warning dream,
> Kind heaven did send to me,
> To save me from a drunkard's grave,
> From want and miseree.

And this was the dream that heaven was so kind as to send him. He dreams he comes home, and the house is in hullabaloo and the wife dead in the bed:

> Poor thing she's dead, the neighbours cried,
> She led a wretched life,
> For want and misery broke her heart
> To be a drunkard's wife.

But he refuses to believe the good neighbours:

> She is not dead, I, frantic, cried,
> And rushed to where she lay . . .

Do you follow me so far? That word, frantic, had not yet entered my vocabulary: and I kept wondering what that placid, celestial figure, Frantie, was doing in the middle of that hell-upon-earth.

Ah well, the drunkard woke up and sobered up and in due course, I extended my knowledge of the English language and found out that 'frantie' and 'frantic' were not the same word, nor person. Give life long enough and it will solve all your problems, even the problem of keeping alive.

In my lifetime I can think of only one footballer who may genuinely have, for a period, established a hairstyle. That was the renowned Dixie Dean who, in the Thirties, played centreforward for Everton and who, it was said, wore the same pair of football boots for eleven years. They made boots out of leather in those days.

Dixie Dean was not, for sure, the only man in the world who parted his hair exactly up the middle, oiled it well and sleeked it down the sides: as far away as Hollywood Joe E. Brown, with a smile as wide as Barnesmore Gap, was doing something similar. But in the world in which we lived, Dixie was certainly the most important man who adopted that style and, to the best of our ability and pocket-money, and to the extent of the tolerance of our parents for greasy pillowslips and the odour of cheap brilliantine, we emulated him.

It was a streamlined style. Utterly unlike the long locks of a later day. We may have fancied that the streamlining would help us when we hopped out on to the football field.

Dixie Dean may have been the best centreforward of his time. Striker, they call it now. He was certainly one of the greatest of all soccer footballers, and the only men whose names would now ring as loudly as his in my memory would be those of Alec James who then played for Glasgow Celtic, Jimmy Kelly who was outside-left for Derry City, Joe Bambrick, the Linfield, Belfast, centreforward who scored a double hat-trick, six goals in a row, against Wales, Davy Martin who went to Wolverhampton Wanderers but who later had cartilege trouble, Mathew Doherty and John Gormley already mentioned, Jimmy Dunne of Shamrock Rovers: Stevenson, Coulter and Alec Cooke, all Irishmen who also played for Everton, and that great centrehalf, Mickey Hamill.

As for the hairstyle in itself and the substance that sustained it: in the days of Charles Dickens the gilded young men kept their hair in order with something that Dickens called bear's grease. For the sake of the pillowslips and the noses of the neighbours, one can only hope that it was really something else, and that the name was only a comic or familiar name. We used a brilliantine that came in twopenny bottles, and when the bottle and the liquid that it contained were at rest, one half of the liquid, and thus one half of the bottle, was green and the other half yellow. You shook it before you applied it and it turned a colour that I cannot exactly remember or, if I could remember, could not exactly describe. In later grander days there was, of course, Brylcreem and even Britannia haircream, so-called, as you may have guessed, because it ruled the waves.

But in the days of the worship of Dixie Dean the twopenny green-and-yellow brilliantine was your only man, and one friend I had who was particularly addicted to it. Because why? He liked the odour and the stabilising effect of it? Or because, more than anybody else, he wanted to look like Dixie Dean? And his hair was particularly unruly. He used so much brilliantine that his hair could not absorb all of it and it overflowed: and on the coldest day in December his perfumed forehead glistened as if he were perspiring heavily. He was, in his own field, nor do I intend any pun, a considerable scholar and could, without any obvious effort, give you like a song the status, scoring averages, points, positions on the League table, hopes for Wembley Stadium and the English cup, past history and prospects of every team in every division.

In those days, anyway, when we all combed our hair the way Dixie Dean did, and when we were in our first year in secondary school, the good Christian Brother we called the recruiting-officer paid us a visit. Since we lived in a garrison town where the British army recruiting-officer did still parade in red coat and full regimentals, and a drum to his tail and a trumpet, also, and a bagpiper playing all through them, that was a most irreverent way of describing a kindly old Christian Brother. Particularly since a real true recruiting-officer, red coat, medals, busby, sash and all, live out of George Farquahar, had had recently some trouble with the little girls: and it was lightly said in the town the military authorities would have given the man the cat but that they were afraid to trust him with it.

No, our recruiting-officers were not at all like that. Two of them I encountered. MacCarthy, whitehaired, saintly. Hogan, ruddyfaced, jovial and occasionally with a whiff of the best off his breath. They went from school to school trying to explain to uncouth boys the nature of religious vocation: and, be it noted, not exclusively in the ranks of the Christian Brothers.

They would begin with a brief talk about the nature of Christianity, which did us no harm at all, and about the religious life about which, naturally and supernaturally, we knew a lot less than we did about Christianity in general. Then in an effort to find out what sort of officer material they were dealing with, they would ask each of us to write an essay, about a page in length, stating more or less what we wanted to do with our lives. Oh, some odd essays they must have read, some odd essays indeed. There were jokers and crazy guys who feared not God nor regarded man, nor the Irish Christian Brothers, and who wrote down that they wanted to be everything from electricians to eskimos, from film stars to famous footballers. There were, also, serious fellows who had already begun to worry about the future and who honestly tried to put their worries and hopes into words.

There were thirty of us in my platoon: most of us with our hair brilliantined and parted up the middle: and on this business of the essays we had been well briefed by experienced and canny seniors. To this effect: that while it was not a manly thing to curry favour it would yet do nobody any harm, for a year or two, not to pretend exactly yet neither to deny bluntly that one might not, if all went well, have some leanings towards the religious life. So seventeen out of the thirty elected for Christ and, three years later, one out of the seventeen did enter the novitiate but left after a few years. The harvest indeed was great but . . .

With an effort I could to this day remember my declaratory essay but I restrain myself from complete quotation. There was a fine peroration about carrying the Christian standard in darkest Africa that must have made that most unmilitary recruiting-officer think he had discovered a cross, a good word in this particular case, between Dr Livingstone and St Francis Xavier. Then the seventeen of us having declared our intent, and with haloes around our heads, sat back to reap the profits of our prevarications. They didn't amount to much. The men who taught us, Brothers and laymen alike, must have been more percipient and/or more cynical than we had supposed: and only once that I recall was my flowery essay, and my hypocrisy, of the least benefit to me, and that was by the sheerest accident. It was at a critical moment in a Latin class.

The finger of fate was moving my way and damn all had I prepared: no Latin composition written, no arid rules ready to reel off: *Ante apud ad adversus circum circa citra cis* and onto these, if motion be intended, God alone knows what should be appended . . . Then just before my hour struck the door opened and there stood a messenger, an angel out of heaven, to say that Brother MacCarthy was in the parlour and wished to talk to me to see how my vocation was getting along. It was the mercy of God or of somebody that I didn't go away with Brother MacCarthy that very day, I was so relieved and so grateful.

Two years passed and our hairstyles were still unchanged and Dixie Dean's famous boots were still holding out: his goal-scoring record in one season has never been surpassed.

Part of the theory of our seventeen vocations was that we were destined for what was called the English mission, and the house of novitiate was located in Liverpool. But as the months passed the idea of a novitiate, in Liverpool or anywhere else, seemed not only more and more unattractive but teetotally unreal. The more thought I gave to the matter the more I knew that I did not want to be anything except what I was: and bad as that might be. It occurred to me also that with all our cleverality we had gotten ourselves into a predicament out of which we could not get without causing considerable offence all round and endangering our future stability and peace of mind: and one day, and because of all that, I am walking home, and in great gloom, with that excessively-brilliantined friend of mine. He must have spent a fortune on those twopenny bottles. The part in his hair was the edge of a sword from Damascus or Solingen. The common housefly was attracted by the green-and-yellow perfume of the sweat of his brow so that, like the tall white devil of the plague moving out of Asian skies in *The Ballad of the White Horse*, he may not have had his foot on a waste of cities but he most certainly had his head in a cloud of flies: and, as was his wont, he talked of recent events on the soccer field, the origins, personal histories and idiosyncrasies of the players, which team had prospered, which might be relegated, how much was paid for whose transfer, even about who kept the turf in Wembley stadium, and how.

He was also one of the sacred seventeen and, with gravity and concern, he listened to my doubts. Then looking down on me in a kindly way, he was a head-and-shoulders taller, he said: 'But look at it this way, Benny. Even if the worst comes to the worst, when we get to

Liverpool we'll be able, every second Saturday, to see Dixie Dean playing at home.'

Well, every man is entitled to his own notion of the nature of religious vocation, and of everything else as well. St Ignatius of Loyola himself wasn't all that clear in his head as to what he was up to when he did his vigil at Manresa after his accident and illness at Pampeluna. Yet I often afterwards wondered what my tall friend had written down in that one-page essay. As it happened he didn't go to Liverpool, no more than I did myself, and I only saw Dixie Dean once and that was in Dublin, and he wasn't even playing football at the time, but he still had his hair parted up the middle. I was sorely tempted to tell him the whole story, or later still to write to him when I read this in a newspaper: 'Soccer legend, Dixie Dean, seventy years of age, is to be honoured by Birkenhead, the Merseyside town where he was born. The council are to name a street, Dean's Way, as a mark of recognition to the man, whose fifty-year old record of sixty League goals in a season still stands.'

When I told the recruiting-officer that my vocation had vanished to places unknown he smiled and said that he hoped that, wherever I went, I'd make a fine and honourable man: and at this present day I'd be glad to delude myself into thinking that I had fulfilled his hopes. But from then on and, possibly, as some obscurely-motivated act of penance, I gave up the brilliantine and combed my hair dry and straight back, and I still do with what's left of it. Perhaps it was that two illusions vanished together, leaving behind them only a nostalgic confusion, and always, when I comb my hair, I think with amused affection of Hogan and MacCarthy and Dixie Dean.

EIGHT
_____

The Soldiers and the Spires

B ugles from the military barracks divided the day as do bells
in a monastery. The barracks stood like a medieval fortress on a high,
walled place above the loops of the Strule. The original building still
stands more or less on the same place, but Adolf Hitler provoked the
extension of the barrack buildings across the river to cover a place once
called Pumphill. On the Sunday before the digging-machines broke
the first sod on Pumphill a great meeting was held there to protest
against the partition of Ireland by British tyranny. We were always hell
for irony, had a special gift that way. When Hitler had gone to God or
wherever, and what with the new army, and all, some of the high
greystone walls were taken away, to be replaced by blocks of modern
buildings. With later advances in civilisation the whole ruddy works
had to be ringed with sandbags and barbed wire.

The first military action against the fortress, apart from an earlier and
idiotic attempt to steal arms, was when an active service unit of the
chaps who call themselves the Provisional Irish Republican Army blew
up the septic tank that bore away what the soldiers didn't want any
more. Almost inevitably the action was described as Shitty-Shitty-
Bang-Bang. The only casualty, I heard tell, was the decent Catholic
curator who, until the works were repaired, had a sticky job on hand.
His politics may have been radically affected, if not his religion. That
may or may not have been irony. The enthusiastic young ASU of the
PIRA may have thought that the thing was there to shower rockets or
something over Russia.

That earlier resemblance to a medieval fortress was not absolutely fortuitous. There had been an ancient monastic settlement on that high place, and John Mossey, father of Michael, and a great traditional musician, told me that one of the monks had prophesied that the place where he and his holy brothers prayed and chanted would at some time in the future become a den of thieves. This was variously interpreted to refer either to the British army or to the unfortunate inmates of the old jail which, on the same site, had distinguished itself principally as the place where, in 1873, Thomas Hartley Montgomery, a sub-inspector of the Royal Irish Constabulary, was hanged for the murder of his young friend William Glass, cashier of the Northern Bank in Newtownstewart, ten miles downstream. If you stand up as the bus passes through Newtown you can have a good view into the room in which, with a hedge-slasher and a sharpened file, poor Glass was bloodily murdered.

From various angles the Townspeople looked up towards the barracks and everything that it stood for. There was the simple, straightforward view that saw it as the symbol of imperial dominance. There was an Empire then. But the normal Irish nationalist, whatever exactly that, now that I have said it, may mean, or even the honest-to-Tone Republican of the time, was more likely to cast that class of a cold eye on the Royal Ulster Constabulary barracks, never referred to as a police-station. It then stood at the top of the Courthouse hill, to your left if you stood on the top of the high steps of that classical building, beside the Doric columns and looked down the High Street and Market Street and Campsie to the Swinging Bars and beyond. When all was said and done the military barracks was packed to the gates with Freestaters, as we still called them, or men from the South of Ireland who may have been betraying their country by being there but who all had, to Northern ears, the accents of Leinster and Munster and Connacht, as rich as Golden Vale cream, as melodious as steel on Connemara stone.

When some jokers ran up a Union Jack on the lands of an old patriotic schoolmaster named Maguire, that fiery old gentleman and scholar carried the offending cloth into the Town and burned it not at the gates of the military barracks but on the Courthouse steps, where the constabulary could not help but see him. They did too, but kept discreetly and mercifully within doors until the fire died down and the scholar had departed.

Then there were some people in the Town, mostly elderly Catholic ladies, who thought that any girl who went to a dance in the military barracks was on the red broad road to ruin: Never marry a girl from a garrison town. Well, the world knows that young men from strange places, and all tricked out in uniforms and the trappings of war, have always had whatever it's supposed to take to turn the girls' heads. But with the amount of money the soldier of that time had to throw around him he wasn't much of a danger to anyone except, perhaps, the enemy who didn't show up until 1939. It wasn't until even later, when young men from stranger places and with accents, as many guileless maidens thought, from the Hollywood screen, showed up, that some of the women ran a bit wild. But who could blame them, with all the example of a wild world before their eyes and all its tumult in their blood?

From a novel of my own which I am at present attempting to write I take the liberty of borrowing this passage, relevant perhaps, to soldier-and-girl relationships in the Ireland of the 1980s:

Newsflash: Five men last night in Strabane, County Tyrone, shaved the head of a seventeen-year-old Catholic girl and then poured green paint over her. It is understood that the girl was accused by her attackers of being a soldier-lover. Many a maiden fair is waiting here to greet her truant soldier-lover. The green bald girl was taken to Altnagevlin hospital, Derry, where her condition is described as satisfactory: If I had you lovely Martha, away down in Inishowen or in some lonely valley in the wild woods of Tyrone, I would do my whole endeavour and try to work my plan for to gain my prize and feast my eyes on the Flower of Sweet Strabane.

Back in the 1930s the army blew its bugles and the soldiers came and went between Omagh and Aldershot and India: and, on Sunday morning parades, the brass or pipes shook the windows of old Castle Street: and no young girls were brutally balded and painted green. But Ireland approaches closer to the great moment of liberation and sixty million Chinamen may yet die in the Valley of the Black Pig and our Mother Eire who is always young, dew ever shining and twilight grey, though hope fall from her and love decay, burning in fires of a slanderous tongue, may require, to perpetuate her youth, such symbolic oblations of young flesh. Or, alternatively, there may just be a lot of kinky guys around.

No more parades, as the man said. Yet those parades of fifty years ago all added a bit of colour to the place, and were so meant to do: Join the army and see the world.

Coloured posters on a dozen walls made every feature of the Taj Mahal as familiar on market-days to the Omey boys and the country boys as it was to the man who had it built for a monument to Love. The army was, also, some sort of help to the economy of the Town. Even if your patriotic principles, or fortunate lack of them, allowed you to follow it, the army was a stiff class of a life, yet, for the man who wanted something or anything to do, it could still be better than the street corners of the 1930s. Once every so often the bugles and pipes and drums and brass were louder, more jubilant than ever, when the Indiamen came home from their stint in hot and sinful places, to go on the reserve, to find what jobs they could: and most of them after their service were better equipped to find and keep jobs: and, also, to lean at corners and tell tall tales. They were great men to pay attention to: and my schoolfriend, Joseph Gilroy, said to me in later years, when he was General Manager of the Bank of Ireland: 'We might never have known anything if Pat Hyndman had not come back from India.'

But higher than the barracks on the hill above the river, higher than anything except Scott's flying circus which in those days visited the Town, so high that they were halfways to heaven and indicating to sinners the way to go to get there, were the spires. On the Church of Ireland, a slender sylph, plain, unadorned, good enough for Protestants with no more ritual than a Jesuit in Holy Week. But up above the Church of Rome, or of the Sacred Heart, and thanks to Almighty God and the pounds and crowns of the faithful at home and the dollars of their relatives in the United States, two giants, one taller than the other, to challenge Cologne and out-Pugin all the Pugins, and to show the Prods that anything you can do we can do better. Winston Churchill must have passed this way. It is one of the few things we have against him that he may have had those three wonders in mind, the naked sylph and the encrusted giants, when he wrote about the integrity of the quarrel represented by the dismal spires of Tyrone and Fermanagh: in the face of the collapse all over the world of crowns and realms, and the breaking of nations and the rolling-up of maps. We had never so thought when we looked at those spires: for never anywhere in the world did I meet an

Omagh man, Protestant or Catholic or atheist or anything else, who had not some sort of pride in those aspiring structures.

Seeking the Lord in the days of my youth I heard a lot of sermons under those spires: no better and no worse than sermons anywhere, or from or for any denomination. The few that I remember had little to do with pure religion but that was the fault not of the preachers but of the blackness of my heart. The mission sermons on the sixth and ninth commandments, the one about adultery and the one about, as Wee Jimmy Clarke used to say, with quite unconscious humour, 'covering thy neighbour's wife', were, when you came to that time of life, a sure draw: 'Recall, brethern, when the light of the passing motorcar picked you out in your sin on the side of the road.'

My contemporaries and myself recalled as best as we could but we had not enough of a record to make the effort of recollection really worthwhile. Nowadays the young unemployed sinners can afford motorcars, mayhap even beds, the necessity for which as an aid to fornication can only be regarded as a sign of advancing age in a man and decadence in a society.

One missionary father broke the mould by thundering on for a fortnight about the Protocols of Zion and international Jewry and all its works and pomps: and how all the rulers of Communist Russia were Jews all the time. All their names ended in -ski, which was a sure sign. The preacher, a tall man with considerable presence, was a Passionist of Paul of the Cross. The menace of the Protocols of Zion, whatever they could possibly be, did not seem so immediate in our Town or county. Looking back at it one might be inclined to think that the passionate preacher had been indulging in *Mein Kampf*, but it was a little early for that and the truth probably was that he had only been reading Fr Cahill, a very nice old Jesuit whom I was afterwards to meet and who, on such topics as Protocols and Freemasons, had an apiary in his biretta. Later we were to hear rumours that the Passionists had to do something about that preacher but what the something was we were never to know: lobotomy or tomcat-treating or steeping for seven weeks in the blessed holy water.

Oh, my Bossuet and my Bourdaloue long ago! Some other great sermons echo back to me over fifty years.

That grey and learned and reverend doctor, John McShane, decided that at evening devotions on the third Sunday of every month there should be inserted between the customary holy rosary and the benediction of the Blessed Sacrament a sermon by a visiting preacher, on temperance: not necessarily a passionate or thundering member of a religious missionary order, but any pious and knowledgeable, and temperate, cleric.

For missionary, you all there outside the fold may read revivalist.

When temperance was explained to an old lady in Brook Street, Omagh, she said it would be no good to the warriors who spent their time at the billiard-tables in the hall of the Irish National Foresters who never saw a tree as lovely as a cue. Not temperance she said, would help them but a bullet in the head, one each. A remark parallel to that made to an old friend of mine in the Irish midlands by a crusty old parish priest who had listened, in confession, to the story of my friend's many amours and then told him that while absolution might for the moment reconcile him to God, or God to him, a bullet in the head would be a more certain method of putting him out of pain.

Then on one famous frozen February night there came to preach on temperance the austere Dean McGlinchey of Ballinascreen, or the Townland of the Shrine, also known as Draperstown, away on the northern side of the Sperrin mountains. His sermon was as cold as the mountains in February: and as long as the Glenelly river that at that moment up in those mountains was writhing and crackling through ice. The church was colder still because the heating system, which normally gave out good heat and a smell of old wet clothes smouldering, had broken down. The Dean explained all about temperance and total abstinence, and Fr Cullen and Fr Mathew, and sent the congregation sneezing and shuddering home: and people who had never had a drink in their lives were nipping, to beat the flu or worse, anything they could get, even up to or down to poteen which was successfully made in the Town, and for quite a long period, by a saddler in a house by the river in Bridge Lane.

But let me, for the moment, concentrate on pulpit oratory.

One Sunday morning John McShane himself startled the church by violently denouncing a new political or sub-political organisation which most indiscreetly had described itself as *Saor Eire*. This was the point of his objection. Allen, Larkin and O'Brien on the scaffold in Manchester in 1867, had, as T. D. Sullivan's ballad had it, met the tyrant face-to-face and with the spirit of their race cried out: 'God save

Ireland: *Dia Saor Eire.*' This new political or sub-political movement proposed to leave God, *Dia*, out of the battlecry. In the dropping of the appeal to the Divinity, McShane, with the knowledge of the scholar who had been to Rome and back, saw all the evil masks of the Latin anti-clericalism of the nineteenth century, and he denounced it in a voice that thundered to the organ loft. The old days of druidic or episcopal denunciation had not then completely passed and the learned Republican from his Roman pulpit could use hard words about what he regarded as deviant Republicanism.

His sermon had its echoes in our house on Gallows Hill, for the house was already well-stocked by my brother with the literature, or the illiterature, of the new liberation organisation: and for my mother, John McShane was one of the Two Great Living Authorities. The controversy was long and fiery, but since they were both tolerant people and family affection was strong no irreparable words were spoken. The *Saor Eire* organisation, or whatever, lingered on into the Seventies to be outpassed or displaced, or something, by worse.

The Second Greatest Living Authority was Captain Connors of the Royal Inniskilling Fusiliers, a small, alert man, an excellent flautist in his moments of civilian relaxation. He held strongly that long, woollen drawers, because they had kept him warm at the Western Front, should be worn by all growing boys: and, my mother accepting the profundity of his message, the ignominious garment had to be worn. With the result that a poor view was taken of the Captain by myself until later in life I came to know him and his lovely wife and family, and their house in a corner inside the grey barrack wall. They were Nancy and Pauline, two lively girls adored by most of my peers, and Mary, a gentle girl with whom, in early years, I developed an interest in opera, of all things, so that every time O'Meara's travelling company came to the townhall we solemnly sat through every performance. Mary died young. There were Eugene, my contemporary, and two younger brothers. Eugene was one of the last men alive out of Dunkirk and he called to see me not long after and in my first novel, *Land Without Stars*, I remembered his visit.

After that meeting with Eugene, who had been to hell and back, never again did I meet or hear of any of the family. Except that an old schoolfriend, who is now a learned judge, told me that the Captain had died in Malta. As a Major.

So: there was a sort of a bond between the soldiers and the spires: and once a fortnight the sermon travelled to the seniors in the secondary school and was delivered by McShane himself: and once a week those of us who played football did our gym in the barracks with Corporal Wheeler or Sergeant Mitchell or Sergeant-Major Weir. Tough men, but oddly sympathetic. English voices, sons of England, where are they now?

To the learned senior boys John McShane talked about many things. We all felt his influence. For those fortnightly homilies he had two favourite quotations and, although he was by no means a gloomy man, they were both from Jeremiah:

> With desolation is the land laid desolate because
> no man thinketh in his heart . . .
> Behold the short years pass and I am walking in a
> path by which I shall not return . . .

But one fine day when I must have been looking particularly mournful, Alec Hyndman, brother of Pat back from India, said to me: 'Not to worry, Benny. Dr McShane will be back here, two weeks to the day from this day.'

NINE

The Hands of Esau

At a function in Dublin City, a reception for visiting American students, I hear a young American girl talk about plagiarising: and I remember the first time I heard the word used with that particular connotation, and how odd I had then thought it, that it should be so used. That first time was in a womens' college in Virginia, USA, and one student said to another that a third student, who was not present and listening, was in deep trouble because she was suspected of plagiarising. Now, with the sort of mind that I have, I immediately thought that those fine upstanding daughters of America had discovered some new, most interesting something-or-other, unknown so far in the backward parts I came from. Because I knew of plagiarising only as an offence or a misdemeanour or felony or something committed by writers: and even the very best writers were at it.

Shakespeare, for instance, lifted all before him, and the clever way in which T. S. Eliot took a line here and there from other poets, and turned them into his own, is too well known to talk about. The point is, we were always told, that what the great writer borrowed, he transmuted, improved and, by his use of it, gave to it an added significance: and, since he generally borrowed from authors long dead, there was nobody around to take him to court, nobody was any the poorer and, indeed, the whole body of literature was the better off.

But what could all that have to do with young women in an American college? Nothing: and what they were simply talking about was cheating at examinations or what we, in the 1930s, called cogging: and a good word, since I assume the metaphor must come from the cogwheel which is turned by another wheel and so on back to the Prime Mover and forward to the Ultimate.

But I fear that when and where I went to school cogging at exams was regarded more as an achievement than a crime: some special examples passed even into the folklore of heroic exploit. If you were caught you had had it, yet I knew of instances in which the catching of a cogger turned out in the long run for the best. One man was nailed in his very first examination in secondary school. He had, under the flap of his desk, a copy of *Elementa Latina* which, for more convenient consultation, he had rendered into a loose-leaved condition. He was expelled from the examination but not from the school. But he was so chagrined by the whole affair that he left school of his own accord, worked hard as a mechanic to whom cogs were essential and became a rich and honourable garage-owner. Whereas, undetected in that examination, he might have ended up as a poverty-stricken Latin scholar.

And I still remember my genuine admiration for a senior who prepared intensively for an examination in English literature by having six copies of *Hamlet* under the desk, all open at different places. Unfortunately the supervising Brother smelled the rat behind the arras and, before the examination began, transferred the Bardolator to another desk. As he lumbered away I could hear him muttering to himself: 'Hell to thee, blithe spirit.'

Then there was the biblical scholar who, when he was sealing-up an answer book in the annual diocesan examination in religious knowledge, sealed into it three loose pages of the Gospel of St Mark, a pocket-edition, which he had just carefully transcribed. He did not, as you may think, come to a bad end. No, he became a famous missionary priest in the Far East and taught the Gospel, which he had studied so carefully, in many's the strange place and, under the Japanese, apprehended for the second time in his life, he damn nearly managed martyrdom.

That annual examination in religious knowledge was, I fear, lightly regarded as far as cogging was concerned. It was bad enough where I came from: but a Dublinman I met later in life told me that in the school he went to, there was a teacher who, with the greatest joviality, would say on the eve of that examination: 'Now, boys, if you don't know the stuff, don't forget the number of the page.'

For one thing, the regular teachers had a day off and were glad of it. The supervisor would be a priest from some neighbouring parish who, unless he was a fanatic and had, himself, taught in a college, was seldom a match for the strategems of the scholars. Of the two supervisors I remember, one would sit all day and read the newspapers so that we hardly even knew what he looked like. There was a theory put out and about by some scaremongers that he had made pinholes in the newspapers so that he could spy through them: but since he never caught anybody doing anything that could not have been so. The other man just sat and slept, unashamedly: and it was under his somnolent supervision that I wrote my notable paper on liturgy.

The trouble about my liturgical studies in that particular year was that, for some reason or other, I was never in possession of the prescribed text. A friend of mine, already mentioned, who is now a legal gentleman was similarly circumstanced. It could have been that the money that should have bought the books went instead to Donnelly's Star Kinema or Miller's picturehouse. Old Man River had finally flowed as far as our Town. But honestly, or dishonestly, I cannot remember. At any rate my friend, who was very talented and could open locks with a portion of the spring of a clock, applied himself on the eve of the examination to the press where the books were kept and borrowed two for the duration. They had crimson covers. They were, I also do remember, honestly returned. Then while the supervisor slept we wrote, not of love nor politics, but of liturgy: and, having a fair gift for transcribing and subediting, I wrote a fine paper. But when the results came some time later I was aghast to find that in liturgy I had got no marks at all: and felt fair enough that some shrewd examiner had decided that the whole thing was too good to be true. As indeed it was.

My other marks, though, were not much better and that did puzzle me a bit. Yet when one of the Brothers mentioned the matter to me I expected only that the moment of apprehension was at hand. To my astonishment I discovered that he was apologising to me: he and his colleagues were sorry about the whole affair and they felt sure that I would agree with the decision they had come to . . . And so on, until I thought the whole arrangement of them had gone out of their minds. What had happened was quite simple. The Brothers had suspected that a liturgist and scriptural scholar of my note could not have done so badly, so they had queried the marks downstream in Derry City where the papers were corrected. Somebody Else had been made happy and was, I hope, surprised by receiving my marks: and I, the creeping plagiarist, had got what the gods allotted although, praises be to Thomas of Aquin, John Chrysostomos, and any others you care to mention, the Brothers knew nothing about that. Somebody Else, though, was in the diocesan college and going for the priesthood and if I was agreeable, and in a Brotherly fashion it was assumed that I would be, nothing more would be said about it, because if Somebody Else was depending on his own marks he would never make Maynooth nor raise his hands on the altar of God.

Nothing more is what I said about it, until now.

Chapter twenty-seven, Genesis, Douai version: how Jacob by two dirty tricks codded old man Isaac and cheated his rude brother Esau out of the blessing and the patrimony, and went on to grow fat in the land and be blessed by the Lord. Except that my story seems to be, or could it be, like the exact opposite? Because, you see, Somebody Else who had not the Jacobean nor the Benedictine wit to cog his own liturgy, was an innocent man. He never knew what happened and, to this day, probably attributes the whole odd happening to the power of prayer. It's an awesome thought that he might be right: and more awesome still to think that in afterlife he may, on the foundation of my liturgical knowledge, have become an abbot or bishop or the Lord knows what. At the very least: any time I meet a higher ecclesiastic of about my own age from the diocese of St Colmcille's Oakgrove (a, perhaps, neutral name for Derry or Londonderry), I look at him with interest and a protective brotherly feeling: I may have been the making of him, may have given him the break he needed.

On the other hand I, the guilty one, had not only got away with that business of the borrowing of the books and the cogging, but was left with a strong feeling of virtue, had obliged the Brothers and the clerical examiners and left them to think that I was not only the Boy Wonder of Holy Week but also a model of self-sacrifice. And the other liturgist, who had the enterprise and the technical skill to borrow the books now sits on the Bench and delivers judgment. It occurred to me, even then, that this was a throughother or mixed-up class of a world.

That then was more-or-less the end of my formal education. That made any mark on me, that is. Life and University College and other things came later and did me no good whatsoever.

TEN

Drumquin, You're not a City

From the top of Conn's Brae you can see, far away and on a clear day, to be sure, a blue pyramid and a blue pigback: Mount Errigal and Muckish Mountain on the Atlantic shore. Nobody knows who Conn was: Conn Bácach O Néill, or Conn the Shaughran, or Conn of the Hundred Battles, or some Conn not mentioned in history apart from having that precipitous hill called after him. Which of us dare hope for so much of the immortal?

Since nobody knows who he was, there is no knowing when or why he gave his name to this place.

Did he run up the brae without drawing breath or roll down it when he was drunk, or did he merely live in the vicinity: there used to be the last remnants of an old house in a clearing here in the hazelwood? Or did he build this narrow twisting road that's tarred now but was, in my boyhood, mostly sand and gravel and loose pebbles? When a horse and trap came to the top of the brae the passengers got out and walked and the driver went at the horse's head to manage him down the steep descent. Likewise the passengers, when ascending, disembarked at the foot of the brae because no horse could be expected to pull a cargo up that slope. Carts loaded with bags of grain or creamery cans meant men pushing to help the horse. Today, macadam and the motorcar have conquered the brae, and the spirit of Conn, hiding in the hazelwood, may have the oddest feelings at seeing the formidable hill reduced to the status of any ordinary negotiable slope.

97

*

My sense of magic is not diminished by my having spent many childhood summers in the valley below there. There are many such private corners in Ireland and elsewhere, and I'm told Tibet and New Guinea are full of them, places scarcely honoured with a glance by a horseman passing by on the main road but with their special significance for other people: those who live there and, perhaps even more for their juvenile relatives who come to camp on them for holidays. The place is less than ten miles from the Town but in the days before motorcars were all that common it could have been in another world. It was escape and haven and a refuge from school. Every stone on the road and bush on the roadside were well-known and welcoming friends.

There were and, I daresay, still are big pike and redeyed rudd in those two quiet, spherical boglakes. Long ago I used to puzzle over how in hell they got there, how, like, did they ever hear of the lakes of Claramore. The simple mind expects to find big fish only in big waters and, also, there is something remote and oriental about the rudd and their cousins, the roaches.

Nevertheless, as the master of ceremonies said at the concert in St Mary's Hall in Belfast when he was announcing that Miss Mary Anne McGettigan would now sing 'The bonny, bonny banks of Loch Lomond': nevertheless, there are two of us here at the head of Conn's Brae, myself and a retired official of Her Majesty's Post Office. He is that musical and learned brother-in-law already mentioned.

We turn our backs for a while on the lakes and Drumard Wood and Bessy Bell mountain and the distant peaks of Donegal. We look towards the northeast at the cartwheel of mountains centring on Mullagharn and above and beyond them to the peaks of Sawel and Dart in the high Sperrins. From the works of the Rev. Dr Marshall of Sixmilecross I fall to quoting, as I frequently do:

> The night the win' is risin' and it's coming on to sleet,
> It's spittin' down the chimney on the greeshig at me feet,
> It's whistlin' at the windy and it's roarin' round the barn.
> There'll be piles of snow the morra on more than Mullagharn.

'Great country up there,' he says. 'And I'm thinking now of an odd class of a misadventure I had there years ago. Just to the lefthand of Dart mountain where you cross the ridge and look down into Derry.'

What he was doing that day, as a young postal official, was checking a postman's walk, a routine by which the head-office worked out the reasonable amount of time a man should take for the delivery, so that he wouldn't be windbroken by hurrying nor be missing all day fishing trout or drinking poteen, both plentiful commodities in those places. The post-office vanman who drove him from the Town to the sub-office was a good Protestant called Willy, who left him there, arranged to pick him up at the end of the route, and went on about his own business. Then, after a few miles, he was alone on the mountain and the lark in the clear air, and he was well content.

He came to this glen, Dart mountain above him, Derry ahead of him and far below, and only four houses in the world to be seen. A long boreen led up to the first house. He sat by the roadside long enough to give the hypothetical postman time to walk to the house and back, deliver the mail, drink the routine cup of tea. While he sat, a travelling grocer, a Catholic from an adjacent village, drove up to the house, saluting as he passed. A little boy came down the boreen, studied the stranger from a safe distance. It was then that he noticed the wireless aerial: and this at a time when radio-sets were rare and reception a matter of God's mercy.

Surely, he thought, they have more sense than to pay a licence fee up in this place. What reception could they hope to get with Dart mountain at the back of the house?

But then he remembered that the licence-inspector from his own office would be travelling these hills in a fortnight's time. So he said to the boy: 'Tell your Mammy I'm from the post office and I'd like to see her wireless licence.'

The travelling grocer drove back down the boreen, cheerfully saluted and went on towards Derry. The boy returned to say that his Mammy couldn't find the licence.

'Oh, it doesn't matter. But tell her the inspector will be round in a fortnight. And it would be as well if she had it.'

And walked on along the glen and forgot all about the matter.

Until a week later Willy, the vanman, said:

'Begod, sir, you've started murder in Glenbank. Mrs Thompson closed her account with the travelling grocer and slammed the door in his face.'

'Willy, what in under God can you mean?'

'She says Paddy, the travelling grocer who's a papist from Plumbridge, told you she had no licence and that you asked for the licence at the only Protestant house in the glen and didn't bother the others.'

'Oh merciful God, Willy, and you're a good Protestant man yourself and you know I was only trying to help the woman. Would you for the love and honour of Marconi go up there and explain to her what happened. Tell her the Pope never heard of Plumbridge.'

My father, who had soldiered on far foreign fields, would say when he looked on some poor fellow who was particularly awkward in his ways: 'They wouldn't have him in the Plumbridge militia.'

There never was a Plumbridge militia.

Plumbridge, he meant, was in the heart of the wilderness. Or in the garden of Eden. Same thing?

Yet not so long ago the Provos had a bomb there.

Plumbridge has joined the world. And the new Ireland.

Willy, the vanman, diplomatically did the job and peace, for those days, came back to the glen.

'But,' said the brother-in-law, 'up there in the unpolluted mountain air. You no longer say pure air or clear air. You have to make a point about air being unpolluted. Up there, with only the cry of the moorcock or the bleat of the sheep to fray the nerves, up in places where there are circles of pagan stones older than we know, I nearly touched off a religious war. Right in the middle of nowhere. Is it any wonder that things get out of hand at the foot of the Falls Road or the Shankhill? In bitter bloody Belfast.'

And we turn our faces west again towards the faraway peaks of Donegal and begin the descent of Conn's Brae.

Aunt Kate said it was the McCillions, not the McDaids but the McCillions. The McDaids said nothing since they were not accused. The McCillions said it was the birds.

The McDaids came barefooted from the far side of the Fairywater river, crossing the stream at the Black Steppingstones. Barefooted in the summer. In winter and raw weather they went shod. They were pleasant young people. The McCillions who were loveable and lovely and multitudinous came from this side of the Fairywater, also barefooted under similar seasonal conditions: and on their way to and from Garvahullion schoolhouse passed through the wide-open spaces of the great farmyard or street (sráid) before the long farmhouse of Claramore. What the controversy was about was what, once a year, happened to Aunt Kate's cherries, seven trees of them. The birds, the McCillions said. But Aunt Kate said, the McCillions. Birds had been known to bite cherries. Birds seldom or never broke branches and, in moist weather, even bare feet made marks.

Aunt Kate was mother to her own large family, part here in Ireland and the rest of them, blossoming out in all directions, in the United States. By friendship and courtesy she was Aunt Kate to half the countryside. In more formal moments and, when need required, she could be bloody formal, and because she was a large landowner, she was Mrs Gormley. Down there at the foot of Conn's Brae and the back of Bessy Bell mountain, and around the great estate of Baronscourt where the Hamiltons ruled, the dukes of Abercorn, and over to the towns of Newtownstewart and Strabane and Castlederg there were an awful lot of Gormleys. Like the Ryans in parts of Tipperary they found it necessary to have distinguishing clan-names. Aunt Kate and my mother, Sara Alice, and Aunt Brigid, a spinster, in New York, and Aunt Rose, my godmother, married to Frank McQuade, in Philadelphia, and two other aunts in the States, a Mrs Martin and a Mrs Weldon, and Uncles Dan and Peter who were legends, and Uncle Owen who was twelve miles away in the townlands of Maroc and Garrison Glebe on the borders of Fermanagh, were all of the Múinte Gormleys, which being interpreted according to Fr Dineen's Irish–English dictionary is, I am happy to say: Taught, instructed, educated, learned, polite, good-mannered.

Their father had been another Owen Gormley, a small farmer near the village of Drumquin, three or four miles from Claramore. He died young, from a wetting suffered when walking-to, standing-at and walking-home-from a Parnellite meeting. Their mother, of whom I have but the faintest memory, still lives for me in wise saws and ancient instances and in maxims passed-on and oft-repeated by Sara Alice, who was a great lady for maxims.

In her dotage my grandmother listened to my sister, Kathleen, who
had a quite remarkable gift for recitation. Even to the ultimate of being
able to reel off pages from Walter Scott: the burning sun of Syria had not
yet attained its highest point in the horizon when a knight of the Red
Cross, or whatever. But on this occasion she was not on Scott nor in
Syria but on the repetitive statement attributed by Alfred Lord
Tennyson to some perfectly innocent streamlet in the neighbouring
island: 'For men may come and men may go, but I go on forever.' Not
quite following the narrative, because of age and increasing deafness,
the old lady came to the conclusion that it had to do with some
unfortunate fellow who suffered from a complaint in either the bladder
or the bowel and every time afterwards when, faintly and afar like the
horns of elfland, she heard the poem she would say: 'Poor fellow could
nobody halt or help him.'

She remembered the famine years of the black 1840s. She vividly
remembered and was much affected by the barefooted migrant
labourers, Irish-speakers, from the far stony shores of Donegal, coming
in droves to the hiring-fairs of Omagh and Strabane to be sold like slaves
into agricultural labour on the fertile land along the valley of the Strule,
the Mourne and the Foyle. (Those hiring-fairs endured into my own
time, up to 1939, you could say, when the European powers managed
for six years to provide full and better-paid employment: with certain
occupational risks.)

From the flagstone at her own door the grandmother could see far
away the white pyramid of Errigal and the blue hogback of Muckish,
already mentioned, and raising her eyes to that remote vision she would
say: 'Ah, the poor Donegals. The poor Donegals.' A remark I love to
make to my Donegal friends, whose riposte is to remind me that my
father was born in Donegal, in the seaside town of Moville and in, of all
the buildings in Moville, the barracks of the Royal Irish Constabulary,
in which force his father, a man from Bruff in the Maigue valley in
County Limerick, rose to the rank of sergeant.

Moneywise, landwise, you might say that Aunt Kate married above
herself to James Roory Gormley, a big farmer at Claramore and, almost
inevitably, a forty-second cousin. Or closer. Anyway, Aunt Kate, like
her mother before her, became a young widow with a large family. That
widowhood imposed responsibilities on her and made her into the
dowager who dominated a fair share of that part of the countryside.

As a young woman she suffered from rheumatism and, for the cure, a doctor sent her to take the hot saltsea baths at Bundoran on Donegal bay. With her went an elderly retainer or duenna to guard her against the dangers of the world, and what the wild waves were saying, and what the wilder men might do. That, in those days, was the way young ladies walked out.

Bracing breezes, silvery sands, booming breakers, lovely lands. Come to Bundoran. That was what the advertisement said in the *Ulster Herald*, and elsewhere.

And the morning of the first bracing day was a Sunday with the breakers booming and the bells ringing, and Kate and Susan, the duenna, on the way to holy Mass which, Susan maintained, might, if heard with the proper dispositions, be a better specific for the pains than all the saltsea water, boiled, between Bundoran and Brooklyn. Into the church with them and made their money offerings to the man with the plate and the table at the door: and all went well for the first five minutes. Until: because of the absence of the Latin Vulgate and other paraphernalia then in use in Roman churches, away before the Venetian joker put the whole concern on the skater-board . . . the absence of these things, I say, indicated that they had, all depending on which way you looked at it, bowed the knee in the House of Rimnon. So out with them and back to the man with the table and the plate, and Kate explained: and retrieved their donations.

And the morning of the second day was Monday, and the breezes bracing and the breakers booming and the sands all silver and the lands all lovely: and the man at the door of the saltsea baths and collecting the money was the man who on Sunday had controlled the plate and the table in the Protestant church. Who asked them, with great good humour, if, ladies, you are certain sure you are in the right house today. He lived a long time that man and must have cured a lot of rheumatism, and never forgot those two mornings and those two ladies and, as Benjamin Franklin so neatly puts it, I have ever had a pleasure in obtaining any little anecdotes of my ancestors.

That stately aunt, honorary aunt to ten townlands, now sleeps in Langfield churchyard: 'in the sheltering shade of Dooish and the hills above Drumquin'. Her son, one of them, my cousin, Joe Gormley of

Claramore, a man in a million, a man to sing ballads and old lavender
sentimental songs and to tell stories, a man in love with the land and its
history, sleeps beside her. The sound of his voice still stays in my ears:

> When the roses bloom again down by yon river,
> And the robin-redbreast sings his sweet refrain,
> As in the days of the auld lang syne,
> I'll be with you, sweetheart mine,
> I'll be with you when the roses bloom again.

He had a version of 'The Merry Ploughboy', an IRA song of the 1920s,
a version slightly different from the one we hear nowadays when, that
is, we hear or care to hear it, and, in my opinion, slightly better:

> We are off to Dublin in the green and the blue,
> And our helmets glitter in the sun,
> Our bayonets flash like lightning
> To the rattle of the Thompson gun.
> It's the dear old flag of Ireland boys,
> That proudly waves on high,
> And the password of our order is:
> We'll conquer or we'll die.

He could sing at the top of his form that sweet song about the maid in
the lonely garden and the well-dressed gentleman who, passing-by,
promised her a high high building and a castle fine and a ship on the
ocean. 'They'll all be thine if thou wilt be mine.' He had been with
the IRA in the old days, going through the motions of military training
at a camp somewhere in the Sperrin mountains. But his only story of
frontline action that I ever heard him tell was a quasi-humorous
account of how he and a few bold heroes wandered around a whole
night with a can of petrol looking for something to burn by way of
striking a blow for Ireland. But not finding any obvious military target
up there in the lonely hills they compromised by burning a barn
belonging to somebody who was at any rate an Orangeman. He would
smile woefully at the memory of the stupidity of it all: yet, in all truth, it
was a respectable sort of IRA in those days. Destruction was still in its
infancy, as the man from Bonniconlon, County Mayo, who had been,
in the days of the *maisons tolerées* to Paris and back, said about sex in
Bonniconlon.

Few cars, then. No carbombs. Blowing the legs off girls in coffee-shops had not yet become acceptable tactics. Legitimate targets.

Looking down from the top of Conn's Brae, or of Coll's high hill above the house of Claramore, on the windings of the slow-moving Fairywater, it is impossible for me not to see and hear Joe Gormley. He had read a great deal about the Tennessee Valley Authority and he saw in the draining of the Fairywater (*omnibus paribus*) a clogged river and a reckless flooder, a hope of increased prosperity for the farmers of the valley. He talked so much about the matter that he came perilously close to being nicknamed Tennessee Joe.

He was right, of course, but the local authority was obtuse and there was a fierce haranguing and slanging match in a committee room in Omagh Courthouse, in the auspicious year of Munich. That was before the building of the present palatial county hall, not as yet blown-up, which was so ironically picketed in 1968 or thereabouts by the civil-rights people. The occasion was a visit to the Town and the county hall by young Brooke of Brookeborough, son of that Sir Basil Brooke about whom much may be said. The posters the protesters carried read: 'Unionism works. Inside this building.' The point was that no Roman Catholics, who, *ipso facto*, could not conceivably be Unionists but must, by the nature of the case or the beast, be Nationalists or, worse still, Republicans and sworn foes to the Queen of England, could find employment in that fine new county headquarters. That protest was made just a little bit before the whole situation quite literally blew up.

Anyway: Back to the Courthouse in the year of Munich.

Marching his delegation down again in a dignified retreat, my cousin, the singing man of Claramore, called back: 'You'll be crying out for extra land in twelve months' time when the German fellow breaks loose.'

'Be your age, Mr Gormley,' said the clerk of the relevant county authority. He was a man by the name of Gamble. 'Be your age. Mr Neville Chamberlain has assured us that there will be no war.'

Mr Gamble may have been, I suspect, the only man who thought like that in 1938. Mr Chamberlain may have had his doubts.

The Fairywater is drained now and, before his death, Tennessee Joe had the satisfaction of knowing that, thanks to his reading long ago about the TVA, his own river flowed unhindered to join the Strule and to go north, by the Mourne and the Foyle, to the sea. Acres are now

under the plough that were once only sodden marsh: to the cousin
alone the draining meant the difference of thirty-two arable acres. The
German fellow has come and gone. Up near Cookstown there was a
prison-camp that covered six fields and was full of the fine young men
who marched out singing against England in his holy heilige name.
The curios and children's toys they made during their Irish residence
are still to be seen in the homes of Tyrone:

> How that red rain hath made the harvest grow!
> And is this all the world has gained by Thee . . .

Dooish mountain, brown and bare and purple, and sombre as its
name implies, still lends its sheltering shade to Langfield churchyard
and the graves of generations of Gormleys, Kanes, McQuaids and
Colls, Keenans, McCillions, McDaids, McCrossans, *et alii aliorum
plurimorum, sanctorum, martyrum et confessorum.*

But no Kielys. For the name Kiely is an oddity in those parts. The only
Kielys I ever knew in the North who were not, certifiably, related to
myself were a family in Derry City, two of whom, Val and Fergus,
became friends of mine and their sister Maureen, alas now dead, a
lovely actress who was the first wife of Cyril Cusack.

But there was another Kiely I heard about. He lived in Castledawson,
in County Derry, and owned an unlicensed bull. Séamus Heaney
wrote a poem about him. About the bull. Not about Kiely.

That Tennessean aspect of Joe Gormley of Claramore and his struggle
with the Fairywater I borrowed, somewhat, to help build up another
character in the novel *In a Harbour Green*. Also I borrowed, for a
setting, the use of his house and the land he lived on. What are kindly
cousins for? He knew, and was amused. That was in 1949. And a long
time later and in a longish story called 'Down Then by Derry' I returned
to Claramore. In spirit. Borrowing the title of the story from that
ancient poem about the green flowery banks of the serpentine Strule: 'It
is down then by Derry our dear boys were sailing . . .'

The cousin, or his shadow in the story, is here speaking to somebody
who might be my own shadow:

'Seriously: Look at that sycamore. It was planted here more than a hundred years ago by an uncle of mine who was a priest. He died young, not long after ordination. He planted this tree on the day he was ordained, and blessed the earth and the sapling. You may recall, when you were young yourself, some of his books were still about the house. Mostly Latin. Theology. Some novels. I told you about one of them and you rushed to get it. You thought I said, "The Lass of the Barns". But, manalive, were you down in the mouth when you discovered it was, "The Last of the Barons".'

There was in the Sixties, and in the Eighties of New York City a lively bar owned by a Major Gormley, US army, retd, and, as far as I know, no certified or certifiable relation. His manager was a friend of mine and a fellow Irishman whose father had been a former Lord Mayor of Dublin.

Once upon a midnight that was anything but dreary Major Gormley entered, as he had every right to do, his own premises and discovered that the guest of honour then present was the son of one Sara Alice Gormley. From that moment on the house was at my disposal. Two hours further on and into the new day, two policemen entered, well-equipped with pistols, truncheons and walkie-talkies. From my Irish experience of drinking after hours I assumed that their entry was by way of being a raid. By no means. Their tour of duty ended for the night, or the day, they were in search of quite legal refreshment and were happy to join our company: and when I cravenly suggested that they might shed their guns, that I had misgivings about consuming enlivening liquor with armed men lest, perhaps, some learned and/or academic disagreement might lead to a fatal arbitrament, they were happy to oblige.

The circle widened. Some time close to closing-time, or four in the morning, an elderly citizen who had just entered the whirlpool looked at me most searchingly and told me to, and because of, my face that my name had to be McGovern. Which I denied. But said that it was of interest to me that he should say so, and why did he say so. In resonant Irish-American tones he told me that I was the living image of a Master McGovern he had known in the old country. Who had taught school at Crosherlough in the County Cavan and who came, in the same county, from Glengevlin in the Quilcha mountains where the great river rises from the secret, enchanted, bush-shaded pool of Shannon

Pot: and from that same Glangevlin, he was happy to hear from me, came my father's mother who was also by the name of McGovern. It is notorious that all the McGoverns from Blacklion and Belcoo and Lough MacNean and all the way to Shannon Pot, and down the stripling stream to Dowra, are inter-related.

More drinks then in and on the happy house in the Eighties, and much discussion of names and origins, and of that matter of knowing who and what one really is, and of what mixtures go to our making-up.

From the Maigue river in the County Limerick to Glangevlin in Cavan and then to Moville and Carrigart in Donegal is not a long journey: a lot less than the little length of Ireland. But to the best of my knowledge that's as far as my father's father ever travelled. Nor might he ever have left the Maigue, with all its memories of Gaelic poets, if he had not joined the Royal Irish Constabulary. In which force a knowledge of Gaelic poetry was not compulsory. The members of the force, though, had many other sterling qualities now belatedly acknowledged, sometimes and by some people.

My grandfather's father had made an even shorter journey from Lisvernane in the slumbrous Glen of Aherlow, in Tipperary, to the Maigue, to settle on the land near the small town of Bruff, around which is written one of the loveliest songs of the many songs of the poets of that tuneful river: 'Binnlisín Aerach an Bhrogha: The Sweet Little Airy Fort of Bruff'.

> The birds carolled songs of delight
> And the flowers bloomed bright on my path,
> As I stood all alone on the height
> Where rises Bruff's old fairy rath.
> Before me, unstirred by the wind,
> That beautiful lake lay outspread,
> Whose waters give sight to the blind
> And would almost awaken the dead.

In the aisling or visionary poem the poet walks out and finds the fair lady lamenting the sorrows of the Gael. On one great and memorable day in my life, Mannix Joyce, the historian of the Maigue, led myself and two learned friends along that river: from sweet Adare, oh lovely vale, oh soft retreat of sylvan splendour, then by Croom, and by Bruree

where De Valera spent his boyhood, and on to Kilmallock and, beyond
Kilmallock, to the high place of Ardpatrick where Domhnall Cam Ó
Suilleabháin camped for a night on his marathon northward march at
the end of the Elizabethan wars. And to the enchanted waters of Lough
Gur, and to the sweet little airy fort of Bruff on the top of which Mannix
produced a tape-machine and the voice of Mícheál Ó Ceallacháin sang
the song out over the sleepy little town.

A most moving moment.

The poet walked out and we walked with him. And gazed on the
silvery stream so loved by the heroes of old. And saw, as if in a dream, a
maiden with tresses of gold. And asked her who she was and from whom
descended. Was she the demi-goddess, Aoibhill, come to sadden our
spirits with gloom? Or the woman who brought the legions to Troy? Or
Deirdre, doomed to destroy?

Somewhere down there the ghost of my grandfather might, with ill-
concealed impatience, have been listening to all that. If, that is, a ghost
can be allowed to be anything but eternally patient. The ghost would
know, as well as would you or I or the poet, that the lady was not Helen
nor Deirdre nor Aoibhill, nor Aurora nor the goddess Flora, nor
Artemidora nor Venus bright. But a spirit of faery, mourning the fate of
the Gael and waiting in vain for succour from the Stuart over the sea.

But my grandfather left the faery lady to mourn by the Maigue and
headed North and as far as he could get without falling into the ocean,
meeting on his journey that woman by the name of McGovern. One of
his sons, my father, had a much longer journey to make before destiny
overtook him in the village of Drumquin. And on the morning of a
Holy Thursday when he was seeking to praise the Lord in a chalice of
brandy and burgundy.

That longer journey began, insofar as I could ever gather, in the Royal
Oak which is on the left bank of the Liffey close to what was then
Kingsbridge and is now Seán Heuston Bridge: King George IV being
quite rightly displaced by a local patriot. But the Royal Oak is still there
to bear witness to the truth of my story. Now and again I visit it and raise
a glass to my father's memory. For in its hallowed precincts he struck up
talk with a gentleman who convinced him that for a dashing young
fellow like himself, all of eighteen and a bit, there could be no better
place to be, nor no better comrades to be found, than in a well-organised

group, now no more, but then known as the Leinster Regiment. There were at the time other notable religious orders or bands of angels: the Dublins and the Munsters and the Connaught Rangers. The talkative gentleman being a certified agent of Queen Victoria, who could not be personally present, a small coin, stamped with her image, changed hands to confirm a contract. Long years afterwards, and looking back on years hallowed by youth and foreign sunshine, he never regretted that moment and that meeting.

There must have been a lot of soldiers around the Parkgate then, and all in splendid red coats and, with the Empire and all that was in it, if you did join the army, you might see the world. Or some of it. There were, when I was a young fellow, medals in a box to prove that my father had been there and back. Years later, when I was a young newspaperman, he said to me: 'I was a soldier in South Africa when Winston Churchill was a newspaperman.' Putting me and Somebody Else in our proper places. Those medals were in a box called the Peace and Plenty box, because the multicoloured illustration on the lid displayed two opulent ladies who made nothing at all of displaying their opulence. But which of them was Peace and which was Plenty I could not well make out. And some time in the 1950s I wrote:

My father, the heavens be his bed, was a terrible man for telling you
about the places he had been and for bringing you there, if he could,
and displaying them to you with a mild and gentle air of
proprietorship. He couldn't do the showmanship so well in the case of
Spion Kop where he and the fortunate ones who hadn't been ordered
up the hill in the ignorant night had spent a sad morning crouching
on African earth and listening to the deadly Boer guns that, high
above the plain, slaughtered their hapless comrades. Nor yet in the
case of Halifax, Nova Scotia. Nor the Barbadoes where he had heard
words of Gaelic from coloured girls who were, he claimed, descended
from the Irish transported into slavery in the days of Cromwell. The
great glen of Aherlow, too, which he had helped to chain for His
Majesty's Ordnance Survey, was placed inconveniently far to the
South in the mystic land of Tipperary, and Cratloe Wood, where the
fourth Earl of Leitrim was assassinated, was sixty miles away on the
winding Donegal fjord called Mulroy Bay. But townlands like
Corraheskin, Drumlish, Cornavara, Dooish, The Minnieburns and
Claramore, and small towns like Drumquin and Dromore were all

within a ten-mile radius of our town and something of moment or something amusing had happened in every one of them.

The reiterated music of their names worked on him like a charm. They would, he said, take faery tunes out of the stone fiddle of Castle Caldwell: and, indeed, it was the night he told us the story of the stone fiddle and the drowned fiddler, and recited for us the inscription carved on the fiddle in memory of the fiddler, that he decided to hire a hackney car, a rare and daring thing to do in those days, and bring us out to see in one round trip those most adjacent places of his memories and dreams.

'In the year 1770 it happened,' he said. 'The landlord at the time was Sir James Caldwell, Baronet. He was also called the Count of Milan, why, I never found anybody to tell me. The fiddler's name was Denis McCabe and, by tradition, the McCabes were always musicians and jesters to the Caldwells. There was festivity at the Big House by Lough Erne shore and gentry there from near and far and out they went to drink and dance on a raft on the lake and wasn't the poor fiddler so drunk he fiddled himself into the water and drowned.'

'Couldn't somebody have pulled him out, Da?'

'They were all as drunk as he was. The story was that he was still sawing away with the bow when he came up for the third time. The party cheered him until every island in Lough Erne echoed and it was only when they sobered up they realised they had lost the fiddler. So the baronet and Count of Milan had a stone fiddle taller than a man made to stand at the estate gate as a monument to Denis McCabe and as a warning forever to fiddlers either to stay sober or to stay on dry land.

'Ye fiddlers beware ye fiddler's fate,' my father recited. 'Don't attempt the deep lest ye repent too late. Keep to the land when wind and storm blow. But scorn the deep if, it with whiskey flow. On firm land only exercise your skill. There you may play and safely drink your fill.'

Perhaps I digress and repeat myself and quote myself. But his mother had promised, back there on a sunny morning by the Clanabogan planting, that he and we would hear the story of the stone fiddle.

But journey's end, as I said, was on the morning of a Holy Thursday and the place was the bar in Doyle's hotel in the village of Drumquin about which village, and the hills above it, Felix Kearney of Clanabogan wrote in the immortal song that, as you may have noticed, keeps echoing all around me:

> 'Drumquin, you're not a city,
> But you're all the world to me.
> Your lot I'll never pity
> Should you never larger be.
> For I love you as I knew you
> When on schooldays I did run
> On my homeward journey through you
> To the hills above Drumquin.

And the request as I have also said was for a restorative in the shape of that chalice of brandy and burgundy. Not overmuch to expect at the end of a journey that had commenced so long ago in the Royal Oak: and had gone on by way of Longford barracks where the tub in the nightroom overflowed in the morning with what in a previous existence had cost twopence a pint.

On then went, not the overflow but the journey, by way, as above-mentioned, of Halifax, Nova Scotia, and Jamaica and where the remote Bermoothes ride, and where he and some other heroes had plans to make the mainland and march to the Yukon. They never did. Their boat brought them the other way, to Afric's shore which also had gold and other treasures with which private soldiers on a shilling a day had little concern. In the West Indies he had acquired a fondness for the eating of bananas that was to last him for the rest of his life. They were plentiful there, I'd say, and cheap and sustaining and he may have felt that he owed them a debt of loyalty. About his African adventure he would say: 'Never fired a shot. Except once at a black snake. And I never knew whether I hit or missed. But I'll tell you what I did do. I walked six times round South Africa.'

Who, in that most idiotic of wars, was defending what or who was foe to whom, it would now be hard to say. But when it was all over, and the weakness of Empire duly noted in foreign places, it was back for the poor bloody footsloggers to Cork harbour and other ports, and to demobilisation and an uncertain future. For my father and some others that was where the Sappers came in. They were not really Sappers, nor were they qualified engineers. They even resented being described as Sappers because they felt that the country-folk who so-called them implied something nasty which had nothing at all to do with soldiering. As the country-folk, being Irish, most likely did. No: those particular Sappers were simply Synge's soldiers from the ended wars, out of work and, as an alternative to being left to beg at the Town's end, employed to carry the chain for the survey men who were making a new map or revising an older one. They picked up the tricks of the trade as they tramped. They could talk like oracles about theodolites and broad arrows. They were great men to walk. Six times round South Africa proved to be excellent training. The circuit of Ireland was child's play. To the last day he was out and about, my father kept the measured, military step.

And his route from Cork harbour led him by Aherlow, from which his grandfather had walked to Bruff, and about which he could talk forever. Then north to that same County Cavan where his father had been before him, and to Monaghan and Tyrone and back to Cavan and back to Tyrone: names like Stradone, Killeshandra, Virginia, Glasslough were in my ears from an early age and every one of us seemed to have been born in a different place.

But for the moment journeys end in lovers meeting, and it is Drumquin, and brandy and burgundy for the love of Allah. The young lady in the hotel disapproves. And says so. She asks him has he a home to go to. Or a church to say a prayer in on a Holy Thursday morning. But she mixes the elixir and he sips it humbly and leaves and is, he thinks, determined never to return. Until Mrs Doyle, who owns the hotel, meets him on the one street of Drumquin and asks him why she never sees his face any more, and he says he is living a quiet life and to tell that to Sara Alice. And she says: 'Come and tell her yourself.' And he does and, over a cup of tea, proposes.

Ghosts of sappers, or chainmen, sat now and again by our hearth but by no means were they reproachful or mournful ghosts. There was Pat O'Leary, a Corkman. Nothing much else he could be except a Tipperaryman, as in the song about being off to Philadelphy in the morning. By a parallel inevitability he had been a member of the Munster Fusiliers. From the stories we heard about him it seems to have been his grand strategy to turn the Boer War into a nonstop flying farce. Which from many points-of-view it may well have been. His supreme military achievement seemed to have been to persuade a platoon of honest English yeomanry to fire all night long at a waving bush under the impression that they were being besieged by Boers. That story may or may not have been true. (See Henry James and my father

Like most of those who return home after long years of exile she was restless. *Eader Dhá Shaoghal*. Between two worlds. So she lived for a while, now with one relative, now with another, then a while in lodgings with strangers, settling finally in a house of her own in Drumquin. But every Saturday morning she took the bus into the Town and breakfasted in our house just at the time when I was sitting in an armchair by the fire and considering the enormity of *Allen's Latin Grammar*. A book I can still do without. We had a long Latin class on Saturday morning. Considering, I say, *Allen's Latin Grammar* but with my mind on other and better things, like young love and football and trout-fishing and more besides. While I stared at *ante, apud, ad, adversus, circum, citra, cis*, Aunt Brigid talked, and the story of Aunt Brigid and Margaret and myself began to take shape. One morning she said to me: 'Margaret's aunt does not approve of the cinema.'

And later on: 'I doubt if Margaret will ever marry that horrid Mr Craig from London.'

It was, I do remember, a sunny Saturday morning and three hours of school were ahead of me like a smoky, hazardous tunnel. Aunt Brigid's voice came to me as it always did on those mornings, from the heart of some numinous cloud. But I had developed a knack of hearing and answering without really listening. What she said I more or less heard but it was always of something else I was thinking. She talked at speed and didn't much bother about responses. So I said: 'That's a bit old-fashioned, isn't it. Even for them.'

Meaning the bit about the cinema.

And she said something like this: 'They are old-fashioned people. Of Huguenot origins. The father's people, weavers and Protestants who came to Ireland from France more than two hundred years ago. Her mother was real French and very beautiful, it was said. She met Margaret's father when she was a nurse at the Western Front. He was then a young officer in the Irish Guards. They say that she had that grace and charm transmitted down the decades by women of her family, softening the rather narrow-minded outlook which Margaret's father inherited from Puritan forebears.'

Now decades of the Holy Rosary of the Blessed Virgin Mary I had heard about and, when the family knelt down for prayers, participated in. Decades of women was an idea that needed some grappling with. But the odd thing about all this was that in Drumquin there was, part time anyway, a young woman called Margaret, much admired, even if from a vast distance, by myself and my colleagues in classical scholarship. She went to a boarding-school in England or France or Goatstown, Dublin, or somewhere grand like that, and was to be seen only at holiday times, and then seldom, and, as I have said, only at a distance. We knew little about her family background but Aunt Brigid seemed to know it all: and I could readily imagine that whoever reared her or was responsible for her would not be exactly overjoyed to think that she had entered either of the two cinemas that introduced Hollywood to the Town.

One was a corrugated iron shed painted red. The other stood on stilts above something that, in that transitional period of the world's history, was half stableyard and half garage. So that above the music of the songs of the time, about tiptoeing through the tulips and climbing upon my knee, Sonny Boy, and telling every little star just how sweet I think you are, you could hear the stamping of hooves and the thunderous backfiring of primitive engines. Certainly the Margaret that we, the Latin scholars, dreamed of had never been seen in those places: so that, Saturday after Saturday, I was prepared to go on listening to Aunt Brigid talking of the villainous insistence of Mr Craig from London who wanted to marry a beauty so much younger than himself. Or talking of the tyranny of that Huguenot aunt. Or talking, and I listened or half-listened to this with a certain indignation not only on my own behalf but on that of my peers, of an army-officer with whom Margaret had fallen in love. But they could meet, I was told, only in secret.

The one morning Aunt Brigid said: 'Margaret has run away to Belgium. Away to Belgium from her beloved Fair Hill.'

And I came awake and realised what was happening. This was it.

Annie M. P. Smithson was a gentle lady and sentimental novelist of the time. See, if you can find them: *Wicklow Heather*, *Her Irish Heritage*, *The Walk of a Queen*, *The Weldons of Tibradden*. And many more and among them, *Margaret of Fair Hill* then running as a serial in *The Far East*, which was not a place but a periodical produced by the Columban Fathers of the Maynooth Mission to China. Aunt B. was following that serial with devotion and giving me, week after week and in *précis*, the instalment she had just read. She had been talking of one Margaret. I had been thinking of another.

In the 1940s I met the only creator of Margaret of Fair Hill: in the

She was buried in the parish where she and my mother and Owen the Lilter came from. And buried on the worst day that God ever sent: low clouds, driving rain and a northeast wind would skin an otter. There was a second cousin of mine at the funeral who, when the good lady died, was on an oil-tanker in the Persian Gulf. The company flew him back to pay his respects. Which was decent of the company. But neglected to dress him for the occasion: and there he stood in a tropical suit, shuddering in the churchporch that was as cold as a dungeon. We took him from the churchyard gate and across the road to the publichouse, and bought him hot whiskey, and borrowed for him a topcoat, and did our best to keep the life in him. He was the coldest man that I ever saw at an Irish funeral.

But what I was really writing about was the funeral of Aunt Rose who loved the woods and leaves of Virginia, and the Blue Ridge mountains: and who was never to see Dublin.

ELEVEN

Some Poets and the Rats' Pad

Melodeon music always reminds me of Claramore.

There were many melodeons about that house, and long dances in the evenings.

One journey back from Claramore to the Town I particularly remember. It was high summer. It was about sixty years ago. Two female cousins convoyed my mother and myself to the top of Conn's Brae and on to the exact and enchanted spot where, on a famous occasion, the left front wheel of John Joe Harte's hackney-car had detached itself from the main body and gone, crashing like a groundhog, down through the steep woods to end up, spinning round and round for five minutes, before Big Mick Gormley's farmhouse. John Joe, who followed his property as best and fast as he could, swore to God and man that the devil or the Good People had something to do with that wheel.

But my mother and myself followed not the path of the faery wheel but the dust road, from the place where the wheel had gone demented, to Clohogue, or the stony place, and on to the tarred road and the clipclop of horsehooves, and Mr McCrumlish, the tea-traveller, and his tilted springvan, aromatic with tea. High over the horse then were the two of us, with McCrumlish, on a wooden seat, and on towards the Town. By Gillygooley crossroads where the Orangemen practised the pipes in the long evenings, and over the railway at the Drumquin level-crossing and on to the main Derry–Omagh road, and the high spires ahead. And up what was once known as Clabber Brae but which, because of Macadam, no longer merits that name.

wearing a black clerical suit and a black clerical hat and had been out of the Town for three years so that I was a stranger to him who had not been that length of time in the parish of Killyclogher. The hat and the suit were relics, apt word, of that year spent in a Jesuit novitiate in Emo Park in the midlands. The black jacket was a bad fit. Because not only had it to cover the upper half of me but to cover also a curious contraption known as a backsplint. The only other men I ever met who had for a while worn a similar sort of harness were President John F. Kennedy of the United States, and Mr Cadwallader, not the ancient hero but a fine man of our own time who was harbour-master and station-master in Holyhead, Isle of Anglesey. My backsplint was the relic of those eighteen months spent in orthopaedic. For five or six years I wore the thing and grew quite fond of it and am now half-sorry that I didn't keep it to hang on the wall like armour honourably laid aside.

It might be possible to say that the black jacket was the only jacket I possessed but then that would not be the total truth. The battered tweeds and serges and school-blazers that had served me in my unredeemed days and before I took off for my brief flight in the upper air and the pursuit of the third degree of humility and the prayer of quiet, had long gone to the ragbag. The brother had rightaway offered to refit me in a manner suitable for civilian or secular life. But he had already paid my hospital bills and that seemed to me to be quite enough for the moment. But there was another jacket, also black, a long-tailed Chesterfield which was part of the novitiate uniform but only to be worn when three novices would walk from Emo Park to that Mountmellick Workhouse, so then still called, to visit the sick. The Chesterfield was called the Tullamore because when the novitiate had been at Tullabeg, in County Offaly, the workhouse visited was in the town of Tullamore. Lord Chesterfield, who believed in smiling but not in laughter, might or might not have been amused.

At any rate, I once possessed a Chesterfield or a Tullamore, tails and all. Few men can make such a boast. What happened to it, and the tails? Where are they now?

So there I was, as black as midnight and my backsplint creaking like a Clydesdale, and there was Father Paul: and the shadow of war was over the world and even over the three rural roads that went out from the Swinging Bars. Over that summer Paul and myself walked a lot on those roads. And became close friends. He came from a mountainy part of

North Tyrone where it was a proud boast with some strong farming people that they had had a priest in the family in every generation for three hundred years. He was a literary man, but a puritan, and when he quoted Burns, which he did quite frequently, it was most likely to be the moralising Burns, assuring me, and the Killyclogher woods and streams, that pleasures were like poppies spread (those singing girls) and that when you plucked the flower the bloom was dead.

Times, his parochial duties required a motorcar, a hired hackney: the war was on and cars and petrol scarce. Required, also, journeys up into the foothills of the Sperrins and in and around the village of Mountfield. In a coomb above Mountfield an enterprising landlord (one of the Archdales, I think) had once stocked a dark, deep lake with Californian rainbow trout. The lord had gone the way of lords and ladies and ordinary misters and mistresses, but the Californian strangers still flourished and the local anglers and poachers had a fine time.

One day, passing through Mountfield, Paul said to me that there was somebody he wanted me to meet, a great lady and a poet, the two in one. The driver of the hackney, without further instructions, knew the way. It was for Paul, the priest, an appropriate routine to pay his respects to that great lady who was also a poet.

We swung left into an avenue. Fine old stone gateposts topped by stone urns or eagles (I forget which), but the rusty gates were open, and limped and sagged. Then along that avenue, grassgrown, and round a bend to confront a house that was finely proportioned but badly in need of the paintbrush. Once, twice, thrice, Paul knocked the ponderous, (what else?) knocker, then roared at the top of his voice: 'Alice, where art thou?'

And the door creaked open and Alice came forth.

The country people said that if you met her on the road you'd give her a penny, mistaking her, perhaps, for Pádraic Colum's Old Woman of the Roads:

> And I am praying to God on high,
> And I am praying Him, night and day,
> For a little house, a house of my own,
> Out of the wind and the rain's way.

But unlike the old woman of Pádraic's poem she had a house of her

country and her countrymen with the exception, or so it then seemed,
of Paul and myself, and the Campbells of Carrickmore who had once
sheltered De Valera, and of some relatives of hers over east by the Bann
river:

> The glamour of the end attic, the smell of old
> Leather trunks – Perdita, where have you been
> Hiding all these years?

A long time ago she had been a little girl in a garden playing before a
big house at the Swinging Bars. The house stood in the sharp angle
between the Killyclogher road which led to Mountfield and the road
which we called, elegantly, the Asylum Road and which led ultimately
to Carrickmore: a place, many people held, full of roaring Republicans.
A man of note in the Town used to refer to people as Carrickmores
much as my father used to talk of the Plumbridge militia. The truth
was, though, that the Carrickmores were a talented, dependable,
Gaelic people: and one of the loveliest women I have ever seen came
from that Big Rock and, for special good value, could sing like an angel.
Wrote a poem once to her, or about her. Which you may be glad to
hear, I will not quote. And never did have the nerve to read that poem to
her.

That garden before the big house at the Swinging Bars was most
certainly in the memory of Alice when she wrote her best-known poem:

> When I was a little girl,
> In a garden playing,
> A thing was often said
> To chide us delaying . . .
>
> When after sunny hours,
> At twilight's falling,
> Down through the garden walks
> Came our old nurse calling –
>
> 'Come in! for it's growing late,
> And the grass will wet ye!
> Come in! or when it's dark
> The Fenians will get ye.'

For the ghosts of the Fenian men of 1867 were still on the hills. It was time for all good Protestants and persons loyal to the English crown to be abed. So the little flock of children ran helter-skelter to the nursery fire to listen to dreadful tales of that night in March with loyal folk waiting to see a great army of men come, devastating. An army of papists waving a green flag, and black police and redcoats flying before them.

> But God (Who our nurse declared
> Guards British dominions)
> Sent down a deep fall of snow
> And scattered the Fenians.

As the great gales had scattered the Spaniards.

But the nurse knows that the grisly ghosts are still there, lurking around the place where one road makes three at the Swinging Bars: and the windshaken windowpanes sound like drums, and the children cry to be tucked into bed that the Fenians are coming. All except little Alice who carried, if not a fanatic then, at least, a rebel heart, and who dreamed of marching under the green flag, and wondered that if she prayed to God would He send fine weather.

A happy childhood memory of unhappy far-off things. How pathetic it seems when viewed against the background of the present.

In 1940 she was seventy-four years of age. She was born in the Town into a Methodist family, the daughter of a wealthy businessman who was also a scholar and a member of the Royal Irish Academy: but born also well away from that romantic Irish nationalism to which she was to cross over with an enthusiasm that marked several ladies of her class and time. Real twenty-four-carat ladies, long skirts and wild, pure passions. Miss Gonne with that proud look aforementioned and all that lovely body, no tittle gone astray. The Gore-Boothe sisters in the light of evening of Lissadell. Anna Johnston, or Ethna Carbery, imagining through the mind of Brian Boy Magee, survivor of the Elizabethan massacre of Islandmagee, the happy day to come when the Gael should sweep his foe through the yawning gates of hell. Tough cutties. In a narrow hallway in Camden Street, Dublin, they or their like lifted the hems of their garments and delicately stepped over the drunken, recumbent body of a young fellow by the name of Joyce. Who a moment previously had beaten on the door, like the ghost of Roger Casement, and shouted: 'Come out, Fay, you can't keep us out of your whorehouse.'

The garden the little girl played in is still to be seen, and the house. In my days it was inhabited by a medical man, a Dr Brian O'Brien who, I have heard, was of the family of William Smith O'Brien, Young Irelander of 1848: who wouldn't lead his revolutionary army across a farmer's field without first asking the farmer's permission. God, if there is a God, be with the good old days. William Smith O'Brien did not, as we may well imagine, make much of a success of the business of revolution. But in recognition of his respect for the law of property he was given a death-sentence, afterwards commuted to transportation. On a pedestal in O'Connell Street, Dublin, he still stands, thinking it all over.

There is in South Bend, Indiana, a lady from the Town who is very much part of my youthful memories. Sometime in the 1950s, because of something I had written and she had read, she renewed our friendship by mail. Her letters, ever since, I have carefully kept. Her power of total and exact recall of the place and the people would be envied by Balzac or Proust or Joyce, or any other tradesman you care to mention. As would also her commentary on the places she has lived in since she left home: London, Wales, the United States. She wrote a most moving poem about the killing of the children by the slagslide in Aberfan, South Wales. My last visual memory of her is when she, a sort of a delicate pre-Raphaelite image, was managing the bookstall in the railway-station, and the Hitler war was on and a lot of British, and other, soldiers passing through. Among them a young poet called Sidney Keyes who became her great friend and who, as we know, was to die in North Africa.

She wrote to me:

I understand that the railway-station is closed now. Only the ghosts of those who passed through it abide there. Some were gentle, some were violent men, morose or happy, ordinary or extraordinary. I had time to watch them passing by. It is pain that they died so young, so long ago.

The young English poet you mention, I knew briefly. He came to buy books. At first he had little to say, simply polite, that's all. Then he and another young man began to talk. They included me. But mostly I listened. It was fascinating. After that, when he came, he talked about books. He asked questions about Ireland. He was uneasy there, considered it beautiful but alien, felt, I think, that the very air of Ireland was hostile to him, the landscape had a brooding quality as though it waited.

He was five or six months garrisoned in our town. They told me he could be very much one of the boys, but he could also be remote. He treated me kindly, teased me gently. But he and a brilliant, bitter Welshman gave me books and talked to me. Sometimes they talked about the war.

It was only after he was reported missing in Africa that I learned he was a poet. But I think I knew anyway.

I never heard if the Welshman survived. I had several long letters from him and that was all.

Now I have a son who will pass through a railway-station or an airport on his way to war . . .

Vietnam was on when she wrote those words.

Some time in the 1960s, before the odd handmedown in the Six Counties of the northeast of Ireland came apart at the seams, Coras Iompair Éireann, our then national transport organisation, had a bright idea: one of many, I hasten to add. Which was to run a bus all the way from Dublin to Glasgow. You stepped aboard in Store Street, Dublin, were driven to Belfast, and onto a boat and ferried to Ardrossan where you disembarked and galloped on in high style to Glasgow. So my friend Seán MacReamoinn of Radio Telefís Éireann had another bright idea: to travel with a few friends in that bus and let them all talk into a mike as they went along, and to tell stories and sing songs, all the way from Store Street to Sauchiehall Street.

So there were Seán and myself, and Sean J. White and John Ryan and Anthony O'Riordan: and in Belfast, and to give the Scots fair warning, we were joined by the poet Hamish Henderson; whom I had only otherwise encountered through his elegy for the dead at Cyrenaica. Somewhere out on the water and to the south of the Sea of Moyle, where the children of Lír endured a swanshape for a hundred

years, I mentioned to him about Sidney Keyes and the Welshman and
the lady in South Bend.

'Alun Lewis,' he said. 'It had to be Alun Lewis.'

Who also died in war.

Souls of poets dead and gone . . .

There are to be many poets in my future, but never another Rats'
Pad.

That Shavian brother-in-law was always a good man to turn a verse or
build a song, comic, sentimental or topographical: and his work
brightened many a parochial concert and, I am told, continues to do so
to this day. And long ago my uncle, Peter Gormley, took off for Canada
in the company of another young fellow by the name of Wilson Guy.
Peter crossed the line into the States, and stayed. Wilson Guy wearied
rapidly of the New World, his imagination dwelt in the past, and he
returned to Fintona, in the County Tyrone, to become, under his own
name, the manager of a co-operative creamery and to live another life
under the name of Mat Mulcaghey, the old besom-man.

For the world that we now endure in, it may be necessary to explain
what a besom-man was. He was a rural type who cut heather from the
bog, or the moss, or the brae, or the moorland: from wherever, you
might say, heather might be found growing. He also cut branches,
slim, three feet or so in length (check against EEC measurement), from
the ash and other trees. Then he tied bunches of the heather to the ends
of the branches and so came up with crude but effective sweeping-
brushes. Then into the towns with him to sell his arts and crafts from
door to door and, hopefully, to make enough to eat on. Style and
appearance were not so important.

In that part of the world there had been a besom-man called Mat
Mulcaghey. There was even a picture of him, old, wrinkled,
bespectacled, and obviously good and as happy as a good man should,
ideally, be. Wilson Guy adapted the name and the picture and may
even have achieved the personality, and under the name of Mat
Mulcaghey he wrote rhymes and told stories and even wrote a regular
column for the local Unionist newspaper the *Tyrone Constitution*.

Which brings me back for one last brief visit to the Rats' Pad, and the
night on which my brother and another good citizen, Patrick
Thornton, went visiting there on behalf of the Society of St Vincent de

Paul. To find one decent woman as good as going with a hatchet for her husband, a thin, most inoffensive man in a coat and muffler, and not too strong in the lungs. So the brother grabbed the hatchet and the lady, in that order, and Thornton, a most polite man, politely asked her why. To be told that her husband, when he got her back turned, was off up in Fintona, chasing about with young rural straps of girls, and that it must be true because Mat Mulcaghey has it all written down here in the *Constitution*.

Producing the newspaper.

With much difficulty they explained to her about the nature of storytelling and creative writing, as they call it in the United States, and that while the name in the paper certainly matched that of her husband, the man who was having the fine time in Fintona, famous for wild women, was an imaginary man. Not her husband who, the brother afterwards told me, had scarcely the strength or the spunk to walk as far as Kitty McElhatton's toffee-apples.

Fifty-seven years ago, and on the day after the event, I heard that story, and much impressed I was by the perils to yourself and everybody else that might follow from writing anything about anybody, real or imaginary.

Then in the 1940s I was wandering a lot around the Clogher valley of South Tyrone, and up and down Knockmany Hill, a mythological place, and through the dark canyon of Lumford's Glen. The purpose of my wanderings was to write a book about the life and times and works of the novelist William Carleton (1794–1869). In Con Corrigan's pub in Clogher town I met MacKenna, the saddler, from Springtown, a few miles away, where he lived in the cottage in which Carleton had spent his last youthful years in the valley before, like Gil Blas, he took the road from Santillane to Salamanca and went out on the world. The saddler had married into that cottage and into another family called MacKenna who had lived there since the death of Carleton's father in 1810. He and his wife Annie became my friends. He died a few years later and Annie remained my friend until her death in 1979. She is still, I hope, my friend.

But on my first visit to that cottage where Carleton, he recorded, had listened to the blackbirds in the hazel glen, below, singing their souls to the rich, cool evening, I encountered another visitor, or two in one, Wilson Guy and Mat Mulcaghey. As Wilson Guy he was also the

resident local authority on the boyhood of Carleton. Pleasantly he remembered that long ago voyage to Canada with Peter Gormley.
   Continuity!

For the length of twelve lines let the Old Besom Man speak for himself about the loving of women and the misadventures of young male citizens of Omagh, the Athens of the North, pursuing the rural nymphs through the fields and thickets of Fermanagh and in the vicinity of the village of Lack (Leac, in the Irish) or the Flagstone.

> When boys from Omagh go to Lack
> To meet their little chickens,
> They leave the road and take the fields
> And that's what plays the dickens.
> For they forget to close the gate,
> And farmers' cattle wander.
> The owner has to pay a fine,
> And that gets up his dander.
>
> Then if a quiet nook you seek,
> And courting you've a mind to,
> You're welcome to the farmer's fields,
> But close the gate behind you.

   The little book from which I filch those courtly lines is called *The Rhymes of a Besom Man*. My copy of it was presented to me, and inscribed in friendship, by Patrick Friel, a most distinguished teacher who ruled over Culmore school on the fringe of the Town and was the father of that most distinguished playwright, Brian Friel. Who spent his early years in Culmore and the Town, but abandoned his citizenship later on and moved north to Derry City and a corner of Donegal. Where he is now the centre of an interesting literary and theatre group. What happened, in fact, was that Patrick Friel moved back closer to his native places, to the Long Tower school in Derry City and the Long Tower Church and those odd, legendary associations with St Columbcille, the first Irish exile.
   A stone in the wall around Culmore school had odd and less sanctified associations, and brings us back to Jail Square and the old jail where in 1873, as we know, Thomas Hartley Mongomery, sub-

inspector of police, was hanged for the murder of William Glass, cashier of the branch of the Northern Bank, ten miles north and downstream in Newtownstewart. The building, the bank, the very office in which it happened are still there to be seen. No patriot, not even in these explosive times, has yet found reason or unreason for blowing them up. Denis Johnston, the playwright, and my dear friend, no longer with us, Philip Rooney, historical novelist, wrote radio plays about that strange story. My schoolfriend, Brian MacBride, who lives in Newtown, wrote a stageplay about it. For a century it was among the most celebrated of Ulster murders. But the times are on the mend and *nous avons changé tout cela.*

A fellow Townsman, Hugh P. O'Donnell, tells me:

One Saturday morning (in the 1920s) some of us, boys, were playing and watching the final clearing of the site of the Old Jail, or what was left of the site after the military barracks had long ago taken over. Big Tim Given, the carter, was carting away the stones when suddenly his horse fell and we all rushed over. The horse's foot had gone into a hole, and, after it was unyoked and rescued and the hole investigated, it tranpired that the horse had stepped into Montgomery's grave. Old Tim reached in towards what was left of the murderer and took out what looked like the remains of a watch, badly burned and scarred he reckoned, by the quicklime. Pump Porter, the contractor, then came along and proceeded to extract a skull which he cleaned and put in a glasscase which adorned his sideboard for many years in Abbey Villa. My sister later bought this house and the skull disappeared on the day of the auction.

The stone on the grave, just a coffin and initials in Latin engraved on it, was built into the wall surrounding Culmore school.

Why, there was even a poem about Montgomery. Author unknown.

> Dark and dismal was the skies
> And thunderstorms prevail.
> These lines I write, for my last night
> I lie in Omagh jail.
> Lonely here, in silent prayer,
> In my dungeon cell,
> Dear wife to you I bid adieu,
> And all my friends farewell.
> I feel the rod to face my God,

> As from life to death I pass.
> With grief I own, the widow's son
> Murdered William Glass.
> Cursed gold, the root of evil,
> Has proved my destiny.
> This day I die in Omagh jail
> Upon a gallows tree . . .

The legend of the thunder persisted into my own time, and as far south as the far end of County Monaghan and into what I once heard Elizabeth Bowen describe as Lower Ulster (a description I never heard from anybody else), the country people would say on a day of wild thunder and lightning: 'That's Montgomery's thunder.'

Ever since I was first interested in stories that sombre story has fascinated me. As in many matters of crime and punishment, you feel there was more to it than ever came out in court. Someday, I still keep saying to myself, I'll write a book about it, not so much about the murderer himself nor his victim, but about the ordinary people who stood around the happening, most monstrous in a quiet place. When I do, I used to say to myself, I'll call the book *Montgomery's Thunder*. Then another man of the name came between me and that title and I feared that people, publishers included, might think I was writing a book about the victor of El Alamein. On whom I am no authority. But if I ever live to write that book I have another and a better title stored in my memory, and facts, figures enough.

Which brings me back by the electric chain wherewith we are darkly bound (Byron) to Frank O'Connor. See that odd poem of his, 'The Patriot':

> Be Jases, before ye inter me
> I'll show ye all up!
> I've everything stored in me memory,
> Facts, figures enough
> Since I first swore an oath of allegiance
> As a patriot boy
> To avenge me maternal grandfather
> They hanged in Fermoy . . .

Frank O'Connor used to say quite frequently: 'Yeats said to me.'

Once, and in my presence, Thomas Flanagan said to Frank O'Connor: 'Michael, what did you say to Yeats?' With vast, all-embracing, good humour, and no man had more of it, Frank O'Connor or Michael Donovan said: 'Tom Flanagan, I said: Yes, Mr Yeats.'

Now this is exactly what Elizabeth Bowen said to me: 'Few of his critics have noticed about Henry James that he displayed all the careful qualities of a Protestant from Lower Ulster.'

Nor did I even say: 'Yes, Miss Bowen.'

I just stored that one away in my memory.

TWELVE

To the Swinging Bars . . .

Iiit was in 1936, the Year of the Abdication, that my colleague Elwood
Greer accidentally put his arm around the considerable waist of Miss
Annie Mullan at the General Post Office in the Town.

'Aughaleague, Aughaleague,' he said, 'Aughaleague onward.'

In honour of Alfred, Lord Tennyson, that remark was frequently
made in the sorting-office in the post office in the Town.

The American letter than Elwood held in his right hand as he stood
facing the local delivery rack was not, in fact, meant for the townland of
Aughaleague but for the townland of Lislap. The Lislap pigeonhole was
on the far side of Miss Annie Mullan who was standing to Elwood's
right hand and was, at that moment, thoughtfully placing a letter in the
pigeonhole whose contents were destined for the townland of
Bomacatall. Elwood, my contemporary and close colleague, was much
too much of a gentleman to reach across in front of the lady so he
reached around behind her, accurately flicked the letter on its way to
Lislap and received a sharp, clean smack on the left ear.

Miss Annie Mullan said: 'How dare you, Mr Greer.'

Elwood's ear rang and buzzed and his face reddened. Reading out
placenames in their alphabetical order, he said: 'Aghee, Altamuskin,
Arvalee, Aughaleague, Augher, Ballynahatty, Beragh, Bomacatall,
Brackey, Cavanacaw, Clanabogan, Claramore, Clogher, Clohogue
and Creevan.'

As he told me later on: 'Damn the thing else could I find to say. To think that that aged dame who sings hymns on the street on Saturday night and Sunday morning could possibly think that me or any mortal man would put his arm around her.'

From the back of the post office you went through the yard where the post-office vans parked, then down a steep, gravelly path and a flight of fourteen steps to a square of matted, uncared-for grass on a sort of platform thirty feet or so above the river Strule. We called the place the Rampart. There Elwood and myself spent as much time as we could steal, leaning on a red, iron bulwark, smoking, spitting down into the flowing water, telling each other doubtful stories, sometimes even singing, forgetting that within the last month we had turned our backs on learning and had become sorting-clerks and telegraphists in His Majesty's Post Office.

There was nothing in His Majesty's regulations at that time, nor before nor since, to say that a postman should not shave nor do his morning ablutions by a bogpool in the townland of Arvalee. The King of England and the men who made his regulations for him may have been too preoccupied to think of that one: and in my brief time in His service there was a postman who took advantage of their preoccupation. But only on summer mornings when the air was mild and the bloom on the heather and the lark singing. Why, his little eccentricity was even celebrated in poetry. A fellow-postman who emigrated to Canada wrote all his letters home in verse, and I recall the general delight when the head-postman, a stout and decent fellow by the name of Willy Somerville, read out of one of those letters these lines:

> On mornings in April, when there is no fog,
> Does Johnny still lather in Arvalee bog.

Across the river, which was wide at that place, fast-running and shallow yet speckled with still pools, and where, on a lucky day, we could be entertained by one of the Town's dry-fly experts wading and casting, there was a greystone schoolhouse circled by horse-chestnut trees. At playtime the cries of the racing, scuffling children came across sharply to us, to me a painful reminder that childhood and youth were gone forever. We were working men now in a working world. Elwood didn't think that way. His father was a country schoolmaster.

'That school over there,' he would say, 'the sight and sound of it gives me the creeps. I'm sure glad that's over.'

But at that moment in the Year of the Abdication I did not want anything to be over. Why, the very first morning I set off to walk from home to my new job or employment in the post office, I had, moving in a sort of trance, not taken the right turn I should have taken. Which would have brought me along the flat, and between the shops of John Street. No, I had trudged steeply and straight up between the white cottages of Church Hill, then around the path by the parish church and so to school, where I had no longer any right to be. School was over forever.

The large playground opened out like a funnel away from the school towards the Christian Brothers' orchard which on a few occasions had been robbed by some really daring desperadoes. The playground was empty, dreadfully silent. So was the rectangular yard between the primary and secondary schools. Classes had commenced. That whole way of life was going on without me, and I was alone and forgotten. Well, not exactly alone. For when I turned, disconsolate, to trudge away to my new life there was M. J. Curry, huge brown suitcase, as always, stuffed with books, widebrimmed grey hat, pinstriped suit, rimless spectacles with a little dangling chain to the right side, planting his feet steadily as he strode along, his broad shoulders as square as the corner of a house, a most revered teacher, tough enough but kindly, a figure of awe, too, because he had once been a famous athlete.

'Lost and wandering,' he said.

'Sort of, sir. Just forgot where I should be going.'

'The books drew you back.'

'I suppose so, sir.'

'Here, take this.'

He placed the big suitcase flat on the ground. He opened the catches with snapping sounds that seemed to me to echo all over the empty and desolate air. He handed me a book. He said: 'It's something new and interesting. I got it in the post this morning from London.'

'But, sir.'

In those days young fellows called their male elders sir. As they still do, I have noticed, in the USA. Or in some parts of it.

'Take this book,' he said. 'Read it. Give me your opinion of it in writing. Then bring it back to me carefully. Don't dare use it to prop up the bedroom window on warm nights.'

That was one of his favourite jokes to students to whom he loaned books: 'Let down the windows and bring me back my books.'

That was, although I did not realize it until long afterwards, my first commissioned book-review: a thought for all who have ever suffered from that most woeful of all literary labours, short of writing a daily column, or leading articles or parliamentary reporting.

What the book M. J. gave me was, I cannot now remember. But I carried it proudly with me to the new place I was going to, and was proudly able to say who had loaned it to me. For all over the Town he was a much beloved and respected man. He once said about me, although not to my face and I feel he may have meant it as a compliment, that I would go far. Because of that statement, reported to me by his widow, he was in my mind when, faraway in Oregon and on the banks of the Willamette river (but indoors and in the university of Oregon, at the pleasant city of Eugene), I was, in 1965–6, going through the motions of teaching. This, I said to myself, has to be what he meant. Not much further can I go, as Francis Drake found out, without beginning to come home again.

Then, ten years later, meditating I was on the banks of the Delaware where better men than me have meditated, and M. J. Curry came back into my mind and heart, if he had ever left them, and I began to write a novella that I called *Proxopera*. The year, as you may have readily worked out, was 1976, and the part of the world I come from, and the absurd political contrivance set up there, by the British and history and ourselves, in 1920, was falling or being blown to pieces. So my novella was about the predicament of an elderly man, a Mr Binchey, a teacher (retired) of history and literature. He lived in a white house by a lake near a town and had his own private stream bordering the lawn and gardens and flowing into the lake: and about how his house was invaded by masked gunmen who force him to drive the car-bomb into his own town while they, the faceless monsters, who have in their mindless minds so made themselves, hold as hostages his son and son's wife, and two children and an elderly housekeeper.

Now, not history had that man taught but Latin and English literature. For when I wrote about him, I was thinking of Michael J.

Curry who came originally from the County Clare and who took his academic degrees across the water. For half a century or so he influenced the lives of wave after wave of men who passed through that school. His mannerisms, his remarks, his witticisms became portion of the folklore of the Town. Between that man and myself, I am happy to say, there was a happy relationship.

It may have been my reading (in Delaware), in a newspaper sent out from Dublin, about the man near the village of Kesh, County Fermanagh, who saw red and turned his bomb-burdened automobile on the gunmen who had so burdened it, and set them scarpering, for their precious, patriotic lives, all the way to Bundoran, County Donegal, that provided my initial impulse for the writing of that novella, *Proxopera*. Humour had thrown an odd Keystonish light on a particularly mean and cowardly form of intrusion and atrocity. But I was also remembering a day in class in the 1930s when M.J. turned from Livy XXII to ask me had I read Dan Breen's book, *My Fight for Irish Freedom*, and if I had so read it, what did I think of it.

Happened I had read it for it was, about that time, almost compulsory Irish nationalist reading. But even though Dan Breen had to be accepted as a Tipperary hero battling in the 1920s against the pretty atrocious Black-and-Tans, my sophisticated secondary-school taste did not give a high rating to his book, not for political but for literary reasons. Don't remember now, if I ever did know, whether Dan Breen wrote the book himself or had somebody do it for him. But it was a crude enough story and not too well told.

M. J.'s objections were more and other than literary. He held it no heroic thing to hide behind a hedge and shoot men in the back. His was an outdated standard of behaviour even then and one that would have imposed an over-rigorous discipline on the devoted guerrilla. Yet when, in later years, I met Dan Breen and found him to be a charming, humorous and human man, it occurred to me, from the hints I gathered from his talk, that his standards did not much differ from those of M. J. Curry. Deeds done in the heat of youth, and not only deeds of blood, seem different to the backward view of age. Naturally I did not raise the delicate topic with Dan Breen, to whom I was introduced by a celebrated Capuchin friar. But in the conversation that followed our introduction, he spoke broodingly of bad times and of things then done that in the time and place he was talking in (Dublin in the late 1940s) would be difficult to justify. He was not speaking only of or for himself.

We have lived, some of us, to see better times and more abominable deeds.

So that it seemed to me, meditating by the banks of the Delaware, an obvious, perhaps too obvious, ploy to place M.J. Curry in the middle of one of our happy contemporary situations and try to imagine how he might react. For the sake of the story I gave him what you might call a false or another identity and background: an ancestry in the town, a son and grandchildren, a white house by a lake. The lake in which, in the novella, the murdered body is found is, in reality, in County Fermanagh. The man whose body was found in it I once met in a pub in the village of Trillick, not many miles from the house I was born in. But the lake I actually describe is close to my own hometown and a comic ballad about it, which I quoted, was written by that Shavian brother-in-law, already mentioned. The white house was there by the lakeshore and may still be there. But the stream at the fringe of the garden is to be found close to Sligo town and in front of the long house once inhabited by a relative of the poet, Yeats.

You pick a bit from here and a bit from there.

M. J. Curry was walking to school on a spring morning in 1939 when he collapsed and fell. The man who ran to his aid was my father. They were good friends. M. J. died not too long after that. Through my father he sent me his best and final wishes. A little before that he had written me a letter. I read it in that orthopaedic hospital in Dublin. He said something like this: That our century had witnessed the horror of 1914–18. That it had left its legacy. That if Hitler, or whoever, started, we would see something worse and it would take a long time to stop it.

For when Bernard Shaw, and other wise men, were making pigs' idiots of themselves, M.J. Curry was telling a secondary-school class in Omagh, County Tyrone, that the dictators, regardless of efficiency and the draining of the marshes, and all that crap, could bring no good to the world.

But we are back, Elwood and myself, on that red rampart above the river Strule, and it is the Year of the Abdication.

'Miss Annie Mullan,' says Elwood, 'will never forgive King Edward. As sure as there's a God in heaven, she's jealous.'

'She is loyal to the Crown, Elwood. As you should know. These days she never lets up about chambering and impurities.'

'If it was only Jean,' Elwood said, 'that I'd got my arm around by accident. Or design. When we're both together dancing cheek to cheek.'

That was his favourite song, as in the Year of the Abdication it must have been the favourite song of a million, and more, other people: 'I'm in heaven, I'm in heaven, and my heart beats so that I can hardly speak.'

Jean was the lovely young woman he was afterwards to marry.

It would seem now unnecessary to add that that post office could produce character, and characters.

At that time the Town was the centre of the largest, or the largest but one, of the postal districts in Britain and the Six Counties. (The other big one was somewhere in Yorkshire.) So there was naturally a great deal of coming and going. Since then, I believe, the Town has ceded some territory to Enniskillen and is, to that extent, a diminished power.

Since those were the days when joining the British army could earn you a free trip to the Old Moulmein Pagoda or the Taj Mahal, twenty-five per cent or more of the postmen who each day walked the coloured parishes of West Tyrone could also have spent some time marching, with measured tread, on the Burma Road or the hot ground of India. There were older men, too, who had suffered belly-deep in the mud of Flanders. Or survived the Dardanelles.

What my brief time in that office gave me was, I hope, a sense of humour, that is, if I wasn't born with one. For from the decent man who swept the floor and tidied up the mailbags, right down or up to the postmaster himself, everyone in the place seemed to be blessed or cursed with a zany humour. Or at least an interesting eccentricity.

There was one stout senior clerk who dressed in strong tweeds and always carried with him a well-bound volume of Dickens, and who kept telling us all that there was a mint to be made by the man who could or would put Dickens on the screen. By several men he has, since then, been proved to have been no mean prophet. He was the first man I ever heard say: scenario. Nowadays everybody says it about everything.

There was another clerk, a man from the mountains of the County

Leitrim, and inside him there was a good horse-dealer trying to get out. His chief delight in life was to buy cheap knives, watches, scissors, pens, pencils, pencil-cases, and all sorts of oddments from mail-order stores, and to re-sell them, at a small profit, to his colleagues. Much more than the profit, which was pathetic, he was in the business for the joy of the bargaining.

And there was, as I have said, Miss Annie Mullan, stout, longnosed, iron-grey hair pulled back into a bun, singing hymns with the Dippers (Baptists) in the Gospel Hall, and outside it, and also outside the YMCA. And it was, as I have also said, the Year of the Abdication and the things that pious, godfearing lady said about Wally Simpson and what harlotry had done to kings, from Solomon onwards, would have made John Knox blush.

And there was a multitude of others, including myself and Elwood, my fellow neophyte.

From our rampart in that old abandoned garden we could watch, also, a tall grey heron fishing in the Strule. After a while it seemed to us that the heron acted very much like a sorting-clerk and telegraphist (SC & T), stabbing the water as we stabbed letters into pigeon-holes. In that process we acquired that impeccable knowledge of the local place-names: Aghee-Dunwish, Aughaleague, Aughanamerigan, Bomacatall, Crosh, Cavanacaw, Clanabogan and on, perhaps, as far as Tummery: pronounced Chummery.

Or was Tummery in the sphere of influence of Enniskillen?

That was fifty-five years ago. The rank, grade or degree of sorting-clerk and telegraphist is now extinct. That does, by negation, give one a sad sort of status. The dodo and other people.

Anyway I left it all and went away to be a Jesuit and, although I didn't succeed in that, the best authorities assure me that the Jesuits are not yet extinct. It might be said by some that they had a lucky escape from me. Or somebody must have been praying for them.

HM Post Office did then, and may still, produce an excellent staff magazine which had a high literary content. That was my (highly-qualified) judgment of it then and my memory of it now. Reading then an article in it, I came on John Drinkwater's lovely little poem about Mamble-on-Teme, the village imagined by him from the sound of the name but deliberately not visited for fear that the reality, seen, might destroy the image. A good poem, perhaps, for walking postmen.

> The fingerpost says Mamble,
> And that is all I know
> Of the narrow road to Mamble
> But should I turn and go
> To that place of lazy token
> That lies above the Teme,
> There might be a Mamble broken
> That was lissom in a dream.

There may be many a Mamble in the life of Everyman. Unvisited. Visited. Or many a Yarrow.

On Yarrow's banks let herons feed, hares couch and rabbits burrow.

In Bridge Lane in the Town there was a pub owned by a man called Yarrow. Inevitably it developed litarary associations. Unvisited. Visited. Revisited.

What's Yarrow but a river bare that glides the dark hills under? There are a thousand such elsewhere as worthy of your wonder.

Thank you, Mr Wordsworth. And so much, also, for the green flowery banks of the serpentine Strule.

But, in history, Yarrow's pub will be remembered as the pub outside which was fought that greatest-ever battle between tinkermen from Connacht and the Royal Ulster Constabulary. For years afterwards it was the done thing, when you were a safe distance from a constable, to whistle: 'Oh play to me, gipsy.' The song had been popularised at the time by Arthur Tracy, the Street Singer, who also, among many other songs, told Ramona that when day was done he heard her call.

> Fair scenes for childhood's opening bloom,
> For sportive youth to stray in,
> For manhood to enjoy his strength,
> And age to wear away in.

At that time, too, I first heard, or read, about the poet Patrick Kavanagh.

It became my custom on my way into work, or whatever, and to strenghten myself against the inroads of imperialism, to purchase from Jamie Boyce, the newsagent, a copy of De Valera's *The Irish Press*, then the voice of Irish Republicanism and, in that year, just about five years of age. Even then, though, the voice had an underground echo in *An*

Phoblacht, or the *Republic*, a paper also taken by my brother and much favoured by those who were inclined to think that Eamon de Valera had joined the long accursed line of those who had betrayed Ireland, that most betrayed of all sad lands. James Joyce thought the exact opposite:

> That lovely land that always sent
> Its writers and artists to banishment,
> And, in a spirit of Irish fun,
> Betrayed its leaders, one by one . . .

But, as Gogol's madman so wisely said: 'Never mind, never mind . . . silence!'

For there is a dogged and somewhat repetitive ballad that follows our history from away back right up into these times, and the last line of each verse runs: 'Ireland's betrayed by Blanky Blank in Blanky Blanky Blank.' The first blank is for the name of the traitor, as and if it fits into the metre. The second blank is for the relevant year of betrayal. Not for some time now have I been in a company in which the ballad has been sung, so I do not know who was last awarded that Nobel prize.

But I am back in the post office: and when the morning's imperial rush is over and the letters sorted out for Bomacatall and other cosmopolitan centres, Elwood and myself withdraw to the Rampart, Elwood to smoke, myself to unfold and read the Republican news. This morning I read on the front page how a reporter by the name of Peter O'Curry, and credit-lines were rare in those days, had travelled all the way from Dublin to the village of Inniskeen in County Monaghan, to interview a young man who had just given birth to his first book of poems, *A Ploughman, and Other Poems*. The poet stepped over the threshold of his father's house and advanced to meet Peter, and used the words of another poet to tell Peter that he (the poet) had been called an idler by the noisy set of assorted citizens the martyrs call the world: and some years later the poet is to dedicate another collection, *A Soul for Sale*, to his friend, Peter, and Peter's wife, Anne. And three or four years after that morning in the post office, Peter is to offer me a job, on the weekly newspaper already mentioned, on which the poet is to be a close colleague.

Ah, fond memories.

*

That journey from the schoolhouse to the post office was my first venture into what we call the world. A journey, on foot, of about twenty minutes towards the Swinging Bars and the northeastern corner of the Town and the Killyclogher road, and the Crevenagh road, and the Asylum road.

From the Courthouse steps down the High Street, and up again, and down Market Street, and on the flat and over Campsie Bridge and the Drumragh river, and on the flat again between the tall houses of Campsie, and on to the Swinging Bars. And back again. And down and up and down again. A gang of us in search of life. Swapping stories, good and bad. Singing, laughing. In search, unwittingly, of life. Practically penniless but mostly content.

There was a legend of a policeman who used to come out of the barracks on a sunny day, slacken his leather belt complete with baton and holstered pistol, unbutton the stiff tight neckband of his jacket, take off his heavy, peaked cap, sit high on the Courthouse steps and look down the High Street and Market Street and Campsie to the Swinging Bars and the woods and hills beyond: and when reproved for his torpor and dereliction of duty he would reply that he had the whole town under observation.

It was a great town for nicknames. What town isn't?

There was Jingle Bells, a pouting brunette and willing servant-maid: so-called because of her unbrassiered opulence and a tendency to jog rather than walk. The American Christmas song was coming in at the time and the words were somewhat altered to honour the lady.

There was the Bluebottle: so-called, and quite unfairly, simply because she wore a bright blue coat. She had not, as far as I ever heard, any buzzing or infectious qualities. She had thin, straight legs that I once heard a streetcorner wit, afterwards killed at Dunkirk, say were legs like elevenpence marked on a new bucket. It was also said that she had been initiated by her Uncle.

Once when a companion and myself were idling on the Crevenagh railway-bank, and hoping for the best, we overheard a row between herself and a rough, redfaced fellow, one of a family of rough, redfaced, fighting brothers. He had a dinge as big as your fist in his forehead where some irritated citizen had once brained him with a wine-bottle.

The Bluebottle was saying little except: 'No!' A mark, we considered, of her ladylike good-taste. But, as she retreated along the railway-track, the rough fellow roared after her that he would tell her father if she did not, shall we say, conform. We considered that to be curious and we were glad when the appeal to parental authority had no effect.

Then there was one servant-maid called Ruby and another called, straight out of border-balladry and Sir Walter Scott, the Fair Maid of Coneywarren. She held court, in pastoral fashion, at the bottom of her master's orchard and bashful shepherds came in throngs to woo her under the blossoming or fruitful or, even, under the bare boughs. Dr Ian Paisley has today a tabernacle or house of prayer quite close to the place.

There was another less-Arcadian handmaiden who passed on to the master-in-reversion of the house she served in, and to his sworn-brothers-sweet, a certain unwelcome ailment. Since the only place in the county in which treatment was then available was east the road in Dungannon, their plight became public knowledge when they were observed to be making trips in that direction. Going to Dungannon in those days meant only one thing, and that had nothing to do with Austin Currie and civil rights.

To protect the young lady's reputation and, perhaps, to preserve her good-will, the young master-in-reversion told his aggrieved father, and the sworn-brothers-sweet corroborated, that the blessing had been passed on to them by a Jewess in health-bestowing Bundoran. All was, almost, forgiven. What hope had innocent Omey boys against anything so exotic as a Jewess in Bundoran? Older and wiser men may have felt regretful-envious that they had not been similarly afflicted.

Then there was the Jennett . . .

A big rawboned girl whose husband was in the Tyrone and Fermanagh mental hospital. She was at home on Saturday nights at the back of a tarred shed in the market-yard, at threepence a guest, which was by no means inflationary, although her earnings on a good night could rise as high as five shillings or sixty pence. Work it out for yourself. She was, literally, a very busy body. She was called the Jennett because it was reckoned that she was hopeless of progeny. This, I afterwards heard, was proved false.

And there were others.

There was Black Mattie, a rural nymph with large flat feet and a sullen cast of countenance . . .

But an aged man must not luxuriate overmuch in the dreams of boyhood. Dear dead women with such hair, too, what's become of all the gold. . . ?

Between the post office and the townhall there was that narrow passageway, frequented mainly by red post-office vans, and in that townhall I did my last school-examination . . .

Now, a recent fit of wandering in the West Country of the neighbouring island, and in the Vale of the White Horse, set me fairly enough thinking of King Alfred and the Danes, and the battle of Ethandune and the ballad of the White Horse and, also, set me remembering that last examination. The connection may not seem immediately obvious.

That last, as I reckon it, examination was in the summer of 1936 and for the dizzy honour of acquiring what in the Six Counties was then called the Senior Certificate. Any later exams, in college or university or whatever you wish to call it, I never quite reckoned as examinations: because in college you were dealing more-or-less with things in which you were interested, with the exception, that is, of first-year logic and Anglo-Saxon.

I'm talking, of course, of my own limited capabilities and of what I was supposed to be doing in college. First-year logic was then designed as an escape-route for students who, like myself, were too dimwitted to grapple with any form of mathematics. In my years the professor of logic was a tall, whitehaired, venerable cleric: and the principal occupation of his students was to count up the number of times, in the course of one lecture, he said 'Ah-Ah'. One lady student set up the record by counting 781 'Ah-Ahs': and since she was the daughter of a notable patriot, and since she afterwards became a Sacred Heart nun, one is forced to accept that she was telling the truth.

As for Anglo-Saxon! Well, that consisted mostly, except for the odd and peculiar person who was going to specialise in it, in learning off by heart chunks of Cook's First Book of Old English: sparkling epigrams like *Hwaet Saeghst hw mangere,* or the declension of *Fisc, fisces, fisce, fiscas, fisca, fiscum.* That bit, as you may have guessed, was all about fish. The decent man who tried to teach us the stuff became known as Fisk. When he found out that that was the case he softened his pronunciation to fish, fishés, etc. Which didn't make things any better, and seemed to me to indicate that nobody now living was over-positive about how Caedmon and the boys did make noises when they came together to communicate. There was a professor in Cork who made Chaucer sound exactly like Harry Lauder. But who is there, or here, to prove that he was in the wrong? Think of Henryson and Dunbar.

At any rate, and apart from codology of that sort, university examinations, as far as I was concerned, were plain and simple, and my last exam, properly so-called, was in June 1936, the month and year in which G. K. Chesterton died.

There was, some years ago, something of a Chesterton revival going on. Why, I do not exactly know. He was never a prophet of doom, and according to what we read in the papers, and according to statements made by this one and that one, and to what we hear and see on something called the Media, we now live in times, even in this misbegotten, fooldriven, bitteen of an island, in which Doomsday is scrawled large on every hoarding and gable-wall. It could be, though, that today more than ever we could do with an extra dose of that special brand of Chestertonian optimism:

> Life is not void nor stuff for scorners,
> We have laughed loud and kept our love . . .

It may have been that the man was due a bit of a revival, as any reasonable writer is now and again, and that he was well worth it. Kingsley Amis edited a volume of the Fr Brown stories, and there were other books, one, by Ian Boyd, on the novels, and a collection of his essays never before published in book form: and I found that I could still read him, and with profit, in fits and starts. But not so as to recapture the first fine careless rapture with which in 1935 I read *The Flying Inn*, and went on from there.

Why or how a boy going to a Christian Brothers' School in an Ulster town should have been attracted by the Chestertonian paradoxes, the wells that shine and are as shallow as pools, I do not know. It may have had something to do with the format of the volumes in which Methuen republished the essays: neat little red books with the author's autograph in gold on the cover. By such considerations are our minds affected. And when I told my parents, and anybody else who cared to listen, that I wanted to be a journalist, I thought being a journalist meant writing an

essay a week for the London *Daily News*, and afterwards having the
essays collected into just such volumes. My mother thought that it
meant covering the lawcourts for the local papers and listening to all the
rural scandals, and spending the rest of the time in the snugs of
publichouses: and later experience, I fear, has taught me that, by and
large, my mother knew more about it than I did.

At any rate, in the middle of that last examination the news of the
death of Chesterton came to me almost as a personal loss. After
Goldsmith he was then my favourite writer, even though Michael J.
Curry tried to turn me off and, perhaps, quite rightly. Firstly: on
grounds of style, because those repetitive and rebounding paradoxes
must necessarily be bad for any young fellow trying to write intelligible
English. Secondly: because during the First World War, M.J. had
grown weary reading Belloc in *Land and Water*, confidently foretelling
from article to article the downfall of the Prussian empire, and it took
four long years to downfall, and by 1936 it was clearly coming up again
and what Belloc, not too objectively, had called the weedpatch of
Europe was spreading fast. Except that this time round it began in
Bavaria.

The examination centre, one of several, was, I say again, in the
townhall. Some years ago I looked at it sadly when the bombing
attentions of some progressive patriots, on their way to the New Ireland,
had left it not exactly fit for human consumption. Since then, I am glad
to say, it has been restored.

But in that June it was a good place to be because the Brothers' boys,
for some delightful reason, were mixed up, for examination purposes,
with the Academy girls, in yellow and navy, who because they were
Protestant were even more exotic than the Loreto girls, all Catholic, in
blue and saffron. Their varying colours I hope I remember correctly.

My next-door neighbour in that test was a fine, upstanding,
laughing, Presbyterian girl who wasn't too happy about the papers
presented to her and who at intervals would mutter: 'Dear God, Dear
God.' While I muttered Chesterton. But when I could, without being
caught, and when I knew anything about the matter in hand, I
managed to pass on to her certain morsels of learned information. As a
result of which, and as a reward for which, she smiled on me above all
other men, Catholic, Protestant, Jew or Presbyterian: and, as a
forerunner of ecumenism, I walked the Crevenagh road with my papist

arm around her strong presbyterian waist. She was a woman in a thousand and later in life I heard, although I can't say if this is true, that she was a blood-relation of a certain noted political preacher.

We drifted apart, as in *Two Little Girls in Blue*, and, although she passed that examination, I never did hear how her later academic career prospered. But I had done what I could to help. Now and again I wonder what she made of me and of that fellow, he must have been an uncle or something, about whom I kept talking, and quoting:

> White founts falling in the Courts of the Sun,
> And the Soldan of Byzantium is smiling as they run.

Or better still:

> The Pope was in his Chapel before day or battle broke . . .

Or in melancholy mood in the evening, and leaning on that Crevenagh bridge over which James Stuart had twice ridden, going to and coming from the walls of Derry, and looking down into the Drumragh river and intoning:

Before the Roman came to Rye or out to Severn strode . . .

But the townhall, as you may imagine, was not built or meant to be simply a centre for school-examinations. Other things happened there. Like the official business of the town and district, directed for forty-one years by a most civilised man, and a friend, John McGale. And before and after him by other good men. Not from nostalgia do I speak but from my burning respect for truth. And concerts and theatre happened there . . . and the Meltonians.

Where the singers, musicians, actors and timeless houris who made up the Meltonians came from or went to, I do not know. Perhaps from, or back to, some paradise east of Suez, Allah be with the days . . .

But seldom up to that time had we seen anything to equal the Meltonians. By the *unco Guid*, and you get a few of them everywhere, and on both sides of what we so happily call the religious divide, it was almost held against the town clerk as a sign of moral turpitude that he rented the hall to the Meltonians. But an appreciative elderly gentleman from rural places said: 'Them cutties are on hinges.' He meant the dancing girls.

Every night of the two weeks they played the townhall the two front rows of seats were, one joker said, filled out with stern presbyterian farmers, hands deep in trouser pockets. They came in, he said, from a part of the river-valley well planted from Scotland after the passing of the Great O'Neill: and where, since then, new ideas and women naked in public had not been too plentiful. A dour, quiet, horny people. But another joker said that the interested farmers were papists from the mountainy northeast where no Scottish foot had ever been planted. A sex-starved, priest-ridden breed. Sex was sectarian.

Nobody in the Town took that sort of talk seriously, nor was anybody meant to. Most people, quite rightly, would not mention such matters. But even the towney Rakes and the bright boys were affected by the Meltonians. To the point of half-a-dozen of them putting a ladder up to the dressing-room window, on the post-office side of the townhall, meaning, perhaps, to enter or, at any rate, to peep. As in the case of Ogden Nash and the rope, the ladder broke and one gallant fractured an arm and another a leg.

Bless us and Amen! The stage in the townhall was meant for higher things than the Meltonians. The concerts with the Loreto girls singing or playacting in those garments of Outer Mongolia, and with lady-doctors from Derry singing about the merry, merry pipes of Pan, I have already mentioned. And myself orating about the Man from God Knows Where. On a higher level, to put it mildly, there were visits from Anew McMaster who taught Shakespeare to as much of Ireland as cared to listen and, in his company, a young Michael MacLiammoir: and O'Meara's Opera Company, which I particularly remember because at a matinee performance of A *Daughter of the Regiment* Vincent McBride, who was my next-door neighbour, but who walked on a crutch and was inclined to be irritable, dropped a lighted cigarette butt down the back of my neck, and the mark may be there yet, I never got round to see.

At the same performance Dick Minnis, that tall Canadian, decided to add some cubits to his stature by putting his schoolbag on the seat and sitting on it, and the crash and smash of his mathematical-set, or box, as we then called it, was heard loud above the music and the singing. And the prancing, of which there seemed to be a lot in that performance. There was Dobell's travelling company and Traynor's travelling company with Baby Traynor, the juvenile lead, playing at hop-ball before the Courthouse, and an object of interest to all of us.

But no, Traynor's company performed in the hall of the Irish National Foresters who never saw a forest.

There was a lovely lady with the lovely name of Dorothy Grafton who played in a piece called *Souvenirs*, and there may still be people alive who could whistle the theme-music or sing the words that went with it. And to raise us to the heights there were, from Dublin, Lord Longford's players from the Gate, and the Abbey players: just once for each of them.

Perhaps it was the memory, lingering over five or six years, of my vast popular success as an orator, and friend and interpreter of the Man from God Knows Where, that caused F. J. Nugent, the director of the town-players, to bend his casting-eye on me.

My stage-career is something I don't often talk about because I have numbered among my friends, I hope, some actors and even actresses, and I get the oddest feeling that they would not be impressed. But, believe me or not, I too did tread the boards, although few theatregoers know about what they were deprived of when my mind was accidentally determined in other directions.

My first big part came my way in 1935 in a play called *Heritage* by Louis J. Lynch, then the head of that distinguished family who owned the local nationalist newspapers. My part was that of an elderly schoolmaster with a frock-coat and velvet waistcoat and a watchchain that would hold a ship's anchor, and on my face a fine moustache: and having passed my sixteenth birthday and acquired a gravelly, broken voice with an astonishing range, from uncontrollable base-barreltone to unexpected bel-canto, I was as elderly, or decrepit, a schoolmaster as you might well imagine.

As well as which I had a daughter: in the play, I mean, not in what we laughingly call real life. She was a handsome Derry woman, a real schoolteacher, somewhere in her twenties, and out of the goodness of her heart she undertook to give me private lessons in how to move about on the stage without falling over myself or anybody else. Those lessons took place in a mildewed room in the parish hall and involved,

inevitably, a certain amount of proximity with the result that, in spite of
the wisdom of my moustache and frock-coat, I developed tender
feelings for my instructress. Nor was there anything wrong about that,
barring a slight discrepancy in ages, and the fact that she was engaged to
a fine man of thirty who was about six feet high.

To this day I am fascinated by the idea that I once had a handsome
daughter who was older than myself. The play, apart from all that, was
quite a success.

In my second and last stage-appearance I was two people, so that ever
since I have had a sensitive feeling for the problems of those actors who
play dual roles. Most of us do that, and more and worse: I'm talking
again about real life. In Acts one and two I was Annas, the high priest,
coming in to tell King Herod, splendidly played by Nugent, that three
strangers had ridden into town.

'Annas,' says Herod. 'A seat.'

The bit about the seat was meant for the Nubian eunuch who stood
by Herod's throne, and who worked by day as a telegraph-boy in the post
office, a lively young fellow who became a famous footballer, and
married, and begot a family: and the seats in Herod's palace were
butter-boxes turned upside down and covered in coloured paper. So
when the Nubian eunuch tilted up one of them to offer it to me, Annas,
to sit on, even the gods in the back rows could read, stencilled on the
inside of the bottom of the box: Shaneragh Creamery, twenty-eight
pounds.

By Acts three and four I had come up in the world from high priest to
wise king for, as you may have guessed, it was a play about the coming
of the Magi: and it was in very stylish blank verse. Which of the Magi I
was, I cannot exactly remember, perhaps the yellow one. But the only
speech of theirs I can remember belonged to the fellow who had come
all the way up, or rather, down the Nile. And he would have to be
black, wouldn't he? As well as which I have a recollection that it was the
man who was painted black who afterwards went on notably to perform
on the London stage, and that, sure as God, wasn't me.

Herod was in fierce trouble at the time. He had a roaring stomach-ache
from which he was subsequently to perish. Then there was all this stuff
about the three strangers and the star and the new King that was born.

All tommyrot, of course, but unsettling, particularly if you had done all the dirty deeds that Herod had done to keep the throne secure. Then the ghost of his slaughtered wife, Mariamne, kept coming and going. Although she was something phosphorescent and stood in the shadows backstage, she was, because of her fine figure, recognisable to all as the Derry girl who had been my daughter when I had been a schoolmaster:

Arms outstretched, Herod pleads with her:

> Oh, answer me!
> Like roseleaves that enrich the dark, brown earth,
> Thy tremulous whispers will bedew my heart.

Fine talk in any townhall. Yet it seemed permissible to think that if he had been all that fond of her, he might have kept her alive when he had her.

And the play, also, was in trouble. The speeches went on for hours until the audience, made captive so as to support, by their admission fees, the ever-with-us church building-fund, were hammered into a sullen submission. There was no natural part in it for the man in the group who was one of the best natural comic actors I have ever seen on any stage. Comedy had little place in the capers of King Herod. So that fine actor (and like the theatrical possibilities of the High Street and the Courthouse steps, he had been highly praised by Tyrone Guthrie) was condemned to pretend to be an envoy from Rome, come all the way to present to Herod a message on a scroll, which was somebody's school-leaving certificate. His approach was heralded by a member of St Eugene's brass-and-reed band walking up a stairway backstage and blowing a cornet.

Then a strap of his homemade sandals snapped and tripped him and the envoy made a flying entrance, landing on his hands and knees at Herod's feet yet preserving his composure as only a real pro could. Only we, in the Court of King Herod, knew that anything was wrong. Not that it mattered because, by Pavlovian reaction, our audience at any play laughed as soon as that comedian appeared and the only few minutes of that splendid drama they enjoyed were the few he spent on his knees before Herod.

The tall, thin, balding priest who had egged us on to do the play said that it was full of biblical lore but that didn't mean a lot, neither to us nor our public.

And Act four was made up of three long prayers in black verse, great stuff for bringing down the house or the heavens.

Curtain rises. The Mother of God is discovered, seated, back to audience, holding a bundle that may be supposed to contain the bambino. St Joseph stands to her right hand, profile to the audience. Enter the Magi, kneel, recite prayers. And in the middle of my prayer I look up to see that St Joseph, a tall, handsome, hawknosed, blackavised man has forgotten to put on his white beard.

Dear St Joseph, meek and gentle, guardian of the Saviour Child (as the hymn addresses him), helped me to finish that prayer, and, since one of my own names is Joseph, I occasionally remind him that for that, at any rate, I am somewhat in his debt.

But then how do we know what St Joseph looked like? Coming from that part of the world he could easily have been hawknosed and blackavised, and the image of Jack McIlroy who owned the Army and Navy Stores, a fascinating old curiosity shop, on the Market Street. The front window of that shop I can still see: old cavalry sabres, gleaming brass helmets and red, goldbraided jackets, stuffed and stiff and up on stands, and tin hats and grenades and the like from a lesser artistic period: all silent and saying nothing about where they had been or what they were made for. Dear St Joseph, meek and gentle . . .

After all that I left the boards to Sir Laurence Olivier and Cyril Cusack and Patrick McAlinney. And others. For Patrick McAlinney, who became a real actor, was the black king who came up or down the Nile and whose lines I can still remember when I cannot remember my own.

And the years pass, and one day I am alone in mighty London, and walking up Haymarket, and I get a strange feeling that somebody I know is watching me. And I look around to see nobody except a lot of Londoners and orientals, and others, I suppose. And I walk on and the feeling persists. And I look up and high above me on a monstrous poster is Paddy McAlinney watching me, his fellow Mage. He is playing at the time in Peter Luke's adaptation of all that Corvo stuff about Pope Hadrian, and shooting the Pope once a night and twice on Saturdays, enough to satiate even the most ardent of Orangemen.

So I look up and say: 'You have clomb mountains, roamed the desert land, have seen the bones of blank, blank, blank that once were living men . . .

Memory fades.

Davy Young's window has to be the beginning of my highway to the world or what of it I have been privileged to look upon. Not a lot. Perhaps enough.

There at that window, and at the age of nine, I stood, having been led there by the brother, to wait for Davy to paste up the notice to say that Lindbergh had landed in France. For all, I daresay, that I comprehended about the matter, Lindbergh might very well have been the man in the moon. And just the other day I hobbled home from Dublin Airport, having come by way of Vancouver and London from San Francisco. Over Canada, Greenland and Iceland, and ice and ocean, and Omagh and Belfast and the Irish Sea and Liverpool, and upon the Midlands now the attentive muse must fall, the shires which we the heart of England well may call, I had as my next-seat neighbour a tall man of Japan who was flying all the way from London to Tokyo. As with Lindbergh, a mere sixty years ago, we landed safely.

Let us not cease to wonder. The crowd outside Davy Young's window wondered and cheered. Somebody played a melodeon. Several danced.

The youngest of my three sisters has another memory of Davy Young's window. I quote: 'Don't be more than twenty minutes on your errand. Don't stop to gossip with anybody. Carry your parcel carefully. Don't cross the street to gleek into Davy Young's window.'

My mother I am quoting. As any dutiful son should. She is, as you may guess, giving instructions to that sister. Nor could the Almighty have spoken more exactly to Adam and Eve when he gave them their heads in the garden. She is sending that sister out the door and down the steps, down Kevlin Road to Tom Kane's corner, along John Street, down the High Street and into the Market Street to purchase in the big, busy shop, run by John Harvey and Jack McGrath, a two-pound jar of marmalade. The instructions might have been obeyed if Kathleen had not met on the way her best friend and near-neighbour, handsome, redheaded, talkative Annie, eldest sister of George and Josie. And Annie knew everybody. Nothing might ever have been known about that meeting if jovial Jack McGrath, jesting with the redhead and the brunette, had not, when wrapping up the marmalade, put a loop on the string that bound it, a fingerloop.

Then if Annie was with you, and you were in any way curious about what was going on in the world, it was difficult to keep away from Davy Young's window. Which was only across the street from the house of Harvey and McGrath: and the combination of Annie, the loop, the world and the window, proved fatal because the loop broke and all the sweet marmalade stickied the sidewalk.

For years and years, the sister says, that marmalade was much referred to.

Davy Young looks out at me, and most benevolently, from a bundle of newsprint that's the best part of forty years of age. It was part of a Christmas supplement to the *Tyrone Constitution*.

Ghosts of giants and of venerable, local philosophers present themselves, unassumingly, in these pages. Davy shares a page with Robert Crawford, historian and antiquarian: and Davy, for reasons too numerous to mention, was, in his practical life, as kindly and benevolent as he looks in that there newsprint, and for me, and for many another, he would rank high among the venerable philosophers. Can it be assumed, for it is certainly to be hoped, that there was, and is, at least one like him in every town.

He was, as I think I've said, a greengrocer, confectioner and tobacconist so that he had two shops, one beside the other, and two windows. But one window, that of the confectioner and tobacconist, was more equal than the other. Because Davy had, also, that wireless set, one of the few that were around in those days. Wireless sets were, indeed, rare and as yet, in their magic workings, but imperfectly comprehended. For instance: up to the northeast in the Sperrin mountains there was, at that time, a man called Ned McCullagh who bought and installed, with the customary maze and complication of wires, a wireless set. No niggard, he opened his doors, or door, and gave access to the new miracle to all his neighbours. From as far away as Dublin and Athlone they heard voices and music and step-dancing feet: Dancing on the Wireless. Most satisfactory. Yet Ned's set had a weakness and one neighbour was heard to say to another: 'That's a poor enough set Ned bought. It said the weather would be fine last Tuesday and damn but it poured rain all day long.'

From what the window ever told us, Davy's set had little interest in the weather, and left hail and shine, and rain and snow and thunder to our own perceptions. But swifter it was than Ariel to circle the globe and come back with all the news fit to paste up in the window. His generosity did not allow him to keep any information to himself. Assorted slips of paper, suspended on trimmings left behind by postage stamps, appeared inside the wide pane. He was famous, all-out, for the football results on a Saturday night. W. F. Townshend, mentioned in heroic verse, and Dan McBride, eldest brother of Vincent who burned his brand on my back, looked after the horses . . .

Farewell then to James the Stuart and to King Herod, and to Davy who gives me his blessing, and to D'Avaux and the ghosts of the troopers camped at the head of Church Hill and on with me down the last darkening slopes of the Market Street, and over Campsie Bridge and the deep, slow Drumragh, then along the flat of Campsie Avenue and all the way to the Swinging Bars.

Once upon a time when we had uppity urban notions there was a bus that ran from the railway-station to the Swinging Bars, and back, eliminating a most educational walk. The railway and, as a consequence, the railway station are now no more. The Swinging Bars, whatever they may have been, were gone long before my time. The name remains, and the place. One road, as ever in my memory, splits into three. To the left, to singing girls and laughing love. To the right for intrigue and dark affairs.

And right in the middle what we called the Asylum road. Madness? So-called not because of the roaring rebels of Carrickmore, for which place that road is ultimately bound. No. First of all the road passes the main gate to the County hospital. Then two miles or so further on it crosses the Camowen and from the bridge you may view the vast bulk of the Tyrone and Fermanagh mental hospital. Times, when I was little, it seemed to me to be as big as the Town itself and I came to the conclusion, perhaps not totally unwarranted, that there were a lot of lunatics in the two counties.

Here, as we know, in the angle between the middle road and the left-hand road is that garden where the little Alice Milligan played in the dusk until her nurse called her in to protect her from the goblin Fenians.

That day when Paul, the priest, and myself listened to old Alice talking through the smoke in the drawing-room in the old Rectory in Mountfield, little did I know that I would live to be a friend of the poet John Hewitt, who wrote that fine poem about his Protestant people on and around the southern shore of Lough Neagh:

> Once walking in the country of my kindred
> Up the steep road to where the tower-topped mound
> Still hoards their bones, that showery August day
> I walked clean out of Europe into peace . . .

John Hewitt was writing round about 1940 when the mainland, Dunkirk to Cathay, was in the horrors, or all about to be, and when that northeastern corner of this offshore island, or nobody in that corner, had yet foreseen the pathetic horrors of the last twenty years.

Three roads before me, all leading out of the Town. To Killyclogher and Mountfield and the hills beyond. To Sixmilecross and Beragh and Carrickmore and the mountains of Pomeroy. And, to the right, the Crevenagh road, going nowhere. Where was Crevenagh? No such place.

But there were other roads.

For one instance: after three or four miles of going nowhere the Crevenagh road joins the road to Dublin. D'Avaux went that way, in middling good humour because he was heading home. James, the King, finally went that way but in a doubtful mood. And many another at different times and in varying states of happiness or otherwise.

THIRTEEN

. . . and Beyond

Here now is where the Crevenagh road joins the Dublin road.

Tradition, that old toothless fellow forever gobbling and gawking over a man's shoulder, tells me that Red Hugh O'Donnell, as a young fellow, passed this way. But he was coming from Dublin, or the little of it was there at the time or the less of it he saw. He was escaping from the dungeons of Dublin Castle into which those long-faced Elizabethan men tricked and trapped him. Just here he was in O'Neill country and reasonably secure. He was on the way back to O'Donnell country and/or MacSwiney country out of which he had, by ship, been kidnapped. Why, the best people in those days, and not only the Persians and the Provisionals, were into kidnapping.

So for a brief while I am tempted to follow into freedom the ghost of Red Hugh: over the Drumragh by Lissan Bridge at the spot where Old Man Tradition has already told us that the living Hugh forded the river, past the Drumragh churchyard where my father and mother and that brother who died young, lie at peace, on through the Town which Red Hugh never lived to see. Did he go home by the hills above Drumquin or further north by another crossing of the big river? Somebody may know. But he did ride on into Donegal, a corner of the country which for me, and for many another has, and has had a special enchantment . . .

For to get away from history and all that I now ask myself a very personal question.

167

When did it first dawn on me that children who grew up in shops seldom had good teeth? Not hardware shops, now, I'm talking about, nor drapery shops nor, and most certainly not, boutiques nor religious repositories. Nor do I mean Confectioners, which is a grand and Gallic description of something or other. No, what I am thinking of is what, in my part of the world, including Scotland, used to be called Sweetie Shops, or shops in which sweets or candies seemed to the innocent eye to be the most notable, and certainly most desirable part of the goods offered therein for sale.

When a child, in that remote time, was particularly insistent on crying out for some of those delicacies, his or her, mother might say: 'But they'll rot your teeth. Look at Little Jimmy Soandso who hasn't a tooth in his head from eating the toffee he steals from behind the counter when his poor mother isn't looking.'

Fair enough, little Jimmy didn't seem to have many teeth in his head or, if he had any, they were all as black as pitch and when he smiled, and who had more reason to smile, he looked as happy as a savage who had dyed his teeth with the juice of whatever jungle nut or berry he happened at that moment, to be chewing. For what were teeth compared with toffee and it was well known that teeth, like apples, would grow again. Every mortal man and woman was entitled to two crops of the things.

My own feelings about this eternal conflict between teeth and toffee, as between ocean and seacliffs, were intensified by my having cousins who had the good luck to live in a grocery shop in the lovely village of Carrigart (already mentioned), in County Donegal, also already mentioned. There they had at their disposal, for their parents were very kindly, easy-going people, everything that the heart or the palate could desire.

To begin with: Gobstoppers. Those were enormous round, hard sweets, as big as billiard balls, which were properly so-called because they did, in all truth, stop the gob and may have been designed to keep a child sucking and absorbed and mercifully quiet for the better part of a day. If it didn't, that is, choke. Then there was Duncan's Hazelnut Chocolate, a Scottish product that was not expensive, yet no chocolate that I have since tasted has ever seemed to equal it.

And there were the Flanagan and Mary Anne Suckers . . .

Calm yourself for a moment while I explain.

These were triangular packets of fizz-powder, each one with a thin tube of liquorice protruding from the apex of the triangle. The odd name was for two reasons. One: You were supposed to suck the powder through the liquorice. Nobody ever did that. You ate the liquorice and then shlupped up the powder.

Two: the product was advertised by a rhyme that began with some mythological Mary Anne singing: 'Flanagan, Flanagan, take me to the Isle of Man again.'

It was some years before it occurred to me, perhaps with the passing away of innocence, that the implications of that rhyme might not be too well suited to children.

Said George, the brother of Josie, to James, an eminent lawyer and bachelor man: 'I am told you meet the best people in the Isle of Man.'

Said James, who spent two weeks out of the fifty-two in that place of happy holiday: 'George, you do not go to the Isle of Man to meet the best people.'

I speak not now of Celtic Man nor of T. E. Brown and his lovesome garden, nor his fo'c'sle yarns nor his gallery of island people: and, anyway, those happy holiday-makers now fly afar to Iberia or the Isles of Greece or to somewheres further east where the best are like the worst.

But back to Carrigart and Bobby Dazzler caramels, or toffees, that retailed at eighteen for an old penny, and retailed at nothing at all when one had the good luck to be holidaying at Carrigart.

Half-time Jimmy came later: a slab of chocolate, firm as a British Square, and selling at three old pence. The package showed a young fellow in football togs rushing off to refresh himself at half-time, although I doubt if even Georgie Best, who was certainly one of the greatest but who never did seem to be over-solicitous about his health, would have bolted such a hunk of heavy chocolate in the middle of a game.

That particular delicacy, Half-time Jimmy, was not available in the Six Counties of the northeast of Ireland, but it was heavily advertised, package-illustration and all, in the *Our Boys*, that periodical much-purchased by students of the Irish Christian Brothers: and one of my first great thrills when holidaying, or camping on my sister Rita, in Dublin City, was to recognise and to buy a Half-time Jimmy in a shop in Lower Gardiner Street. It had been in the shop-window for some time and had suffered from the sun. Yet it was still deliciously edible and as I sunk my teeth into it I knew that I was forever tied to Dublin City.

But when I was holidaying with my cousins in Carrigart they were always kind and helpful, always modest about their riches and unlimited sources of supply: and to this day I wonder how my teeth ever survived the deposits of semi-molten sugar that lodged in their crevices and cavities. The teeth of my cousins, to be quite honest about it, were not so good. Also: no matter how pleasant and generous my cousins were, I still could not help feeling that, because I didn't live in a shop, I was a poor relation. Back at home we had nothing better than a house.

Carrigart, though, had other things to offer to take my mind off my penury. It had the sea: that neat, round, little bay, a suckling of Mulroy Bay, tucked in at the back of the village. It had its distant, well not so distant, view of the mountains, the hills of Donegal (including Muckish), romanticised in song and romantically inspiring in reality. It had the windblown, shortgrassed slopes of Figart Hill, a most delightful promontory. Over a few acres of land on Figart that uniformed grandfather had fought and won, it was said, a lawcase with that Earl of Leitrim who, in 1887, was murdered a few miles away in Cratloe Wood. My grandfather had, naturally or otherwise, nothing to do with the murder, but there is a theory, or a legend, that he was the first man in the uniform of the late Queen to be informed that the murder had happened. The absolute historicity of all this I have never checked, nor ever will. Never spoil a good story for the sake of the truth.

And Carrigart had my uncle, Eddy, who was deaf but who taught me, in a basement kitchen where we lurked, and which nobody else much frequented, how to roast cockles in their shells on a red sod of turf and then pick them out with a pin and eat them: an exclusive dish that I haven't sampled for a long time now. Eddy was a bachelor man who lived with his brother Michael, and Michael's family, my, as you may guess, cousins. And their mother, Michael's wife.

Carrigart even had the memorable Sunday morning when that third sister struck the parish priest's dog: a shambling, longhaired monster who presumed, perhaps fairly enough, that he had some ecclesiastical status and used to go snuffing around the pews and/or benches in the middle of the Mass. Not knowing who he was my sister let him have it fair and square on the nose with the binding of her Roman missal, with results that were disastrous and deafening and a severe distraction to the faithful. That was as near as my sister ever managed to get to sacrilege.

But first, and before all, Carrigart displayed to me how the rich really lived, even if they had to sacrifice their teeth to maintain their life-style: and I was beginning to realise, as everybody around me grew older, that with money you could even buy teeth. But as I say, and God be praised, and in spite of those holiday orgies with my cousins, my teeth have survived so well that a noted dental surgeon once complimented me, or my teeth: and my age and all. Far back and away from the vulgar view, there may be gaps in the line of defence and/or attack, but the front line still holds firm, and I have still kept my sweet tooth although I do not know which of them it is: and although old pennies are no more, nor Bobby Dazzlers, nor gobstoppers, and the woods from which the nuts came for Duncan's Hazelnut may be as dead as the woods of Arcady, or as down and laid low as woods of Kilcash . . .

Walking along Lower Gardiner Street in downtown Dublin the other day I saw with sadness that the shop in which I bought that Half-time Jimmy, and the high old Georgian house that had contained that shop, were gone. And suddenly, Carrigart and Figart Hill, and the priest's dog and the cockles roasting on the red sod, and the expertise of Uncle Eddy as he prised the cooked cockles out with a pin, and my cousins and myself walking by the circular bay, our mouths full of toffees, seemed further away from me than the moon is nowadays, or San Francisco . . .

Then some children, as most of us must know since most of us were ourselves once children, go through hell when they go on holidays. They're a little like cats rooted out of familiar corners. There's a story I loved about a little Donegal girl who, once a year, used to be sent thirty miles along the coast from the beauty of the place where she lived, with her father and mother and brothers, to the even more decided beauty of the place where her mother's mother lived with two of the girl's uncles and the wife of one of them.

She wasn't a little Donegal girl when she told me this story. She was a little Donegal woman, very good, very kind, very practical. You know what they're like in that semi-detached corner of the northwest. When she told me all this we were standing on a great, swooping Donegal headland and looking across a square-shaped bay, and over a lower headland to a glistening semi-circle of surf and sand-dunes, and good grassland beyond all that.

'There it is,' she said, 'over there, my granny's place. I hated every field and every sandhill.'

She hated every moment of the holiday or thought she did, as she looked back. She may have been exaggerating. Yet in spite of those decent people who still hold that children come trailing clouds of glory, we do all know that the memory of one simple, and often silly, childish unhappiness can last a long time.

It wasn't that there was anything unpleasant about her granny or her uncles. Far from it. They were the best people in the world and they would have been horrified to think that she was unhappy for even one moment. But for one thing, she had been taken out of the cat's corner she had made for herself and, for another, she couldn't understand one half of what her relatives were saying. It wasn't their English. It wasn't their Irish. It was their bloodywell Scottish. Because through one of those oddities in the distribution of dialect that you find in Donegal and, indeed, all over Ulster, her relatives seemed to have studied speech with some boatload of Covenanters who came, in Stuart times, across the sea from Scotland to get away from the persecuting fury of Clavers, who could only be killed by a silver bullet and whose name is spelled, in case you don't know, as if it were Claverhouse.

One word in common usage with her relatives was the word: stirk. Over to the east, in Tyrone, I've heard it often. Around Drumquin they used to, and may still say, on a day of downpour, that it's raining bullock-stirks. But to the little Donegal girl whose people, thirty miles away, did not talk Scottish, the word was incomprehensible.

Now every year as soon as she'd get to her granny's it was her bounden duty to write a letter home. Her mother provided her in advance with pen, paper, stamped envelope and a bottle of ink. As soon then as she had washed her hands and face, disposed of the evening meal, and her granny had turned up the lamp, down she would sit, lick the nib, dip it, and begin: 'Dear Mother, I have arrived safely. All are well here as hoping this finds you at present . . .'

And so on. But one year the urge to be a real writer and to comment on life seized her and off she went: 'They have things here that they call stirks. They have four legs and a head and a tail and they look the spittin image of cows.'

Standing then with that little Donegal woman on a high headland, and looking over a low headland to the shining place where the little Donegal girl holidayed, and came for the first time up against the problems of linguistics, I had a vision of all the little children walking in the loneliness that is inevitably created by unfamiliar places: and it occurred to me that we must have been told a lot of nonsense about that ancient Irish institution of fosterage.

Red Hugh O'Donnel may have been one of its many sufferers. He was lured on board that English ship and kidnapped while out at fosterage at Doe Castle in North Donegal, with his relative, MacSwiney of the Battleaxes. But perhaps he was only running away and went in the wrong direction and with the wrong people. He was young and may have been wild for any escape. Imagine living in the house of a man yclept MacSwiney of the Battleaxes. How did you address him when you wanted more?

There is, though, another side to the story. Some wee fellows, for instance, develop a ferocious attachment to their grannies. There's a friend of mine who is now over there in Edinboro, a droll man, indeed, and one of the best ever to sing that ballad about your own father's garden in the County Tyrone. At regular intervals he would explain to myself and others: 'You see, I'm one of those wee fellows who had the ringworm and was reared by his granny.'

This is the way it was. His father was a bank manager in a big town and the boy's health wasn't too good. So he was packed off to his granny in the townland of Magheracolton, if any of you know where that is, where he would grow strong on clean air and country-living. Then at regular intervals the parents would call to pretend to take him back to school. Warned of their visit he would take to the hill behind the house and his granny would hang a white apron in a high dormer-window. When the apron was taken down the visitors had gone and it was safe for the refugee to come in off his keeping. So for an agreed period the happy game went on until the boy was fit and well enough to face back to the town and school.

For myself, I was lucky in my experiences of fosterage, or just especially lucky in my relatives in Tyrone, in Sligo and Leitrim and

Dublin and Donegal, and lucky too, perhaps, in my adaptability or my weakness for wandering.

There is a lingering regret, though, that I never did get the brown donkey that my uncle Owen promised me, up there on his mountain farm by Maroc and Garrison Glebe on the borders of Tyrone and Fermanagh. He was a pretty wonderful man and, as I have said, could lilt and sing and shoot the fish, and was the first to show me hedgehogs on the hill and crayfish in the stream, and he could carve the most wonderful things out of wood, using nothing more elaborate than a huge tobacco-smelling claspknife. But he did promise me a brown donkey and I never got it. Later on I came to see my uncle's reasons: I might have looked odd going to school on the back of a brown donkey, up the steep slope of Church Hill and across the place where the troopers of King James had rested themselves and their horses. And pasturage for my mount might have created problems. But I did miss that donkey and I know now that the most testing thing in the world is to make a promise, and not only to children.

My holidays, all, I enjoyed and they ended, all, in melancholy. Not because I did not want to go home. No, nobody was ever happier at home. Not even because the end of the holiday meant going back to school. No the reason went a lot deeper. It was a foretaste of things to come, a premonition of what, for want of a better word, we call life. Those holidays were absolute freedom and from an early age I fear that I had a feeling that, in life, the interludes of absolute freedom, the green isles in the deep wide sea of misery, were not going to be as many as the poor poet thought, or hoped, they might be.

Carrigart was my introduction to Donegal, that county in which my father was born and reared. He grew up in Carrigart, and the stories he heard and altered and added to and passed on, and the stories he made up, became a large part of my own mythology.

Up the slow slope then by Fintona and Seskinore, where Elwood came from, and over the ridge and watershed, and away from the Drumragh and into the valley of the Ulster Blackwater. Far away to the east, at Benburb, Hugh O'Neill once fought a mighty battle across that river. Tucked in here somewhere in a secret corner is a place called Newtownsaville which I have never seen, never gone to see. My

Mamble? Lissom in a dream. But who could fit Newtownsaville, whatever it is, into a poem? Ogden Nash? Perhaps John Montague. Some day when I'm going home again, contrary to all the wisdom and warning of Thomas Wolfe, I'll be damned if I don't step sideways and take a look at Newtownsaville.

Up here on these slopes, and in the townland of Ballymacilroy, Henry Kelly and Peter Quinn lost in the night the greyhound bitch that belonged to Tommy Mullan, the postman, who also fished in the Drumragh and the Strule for freshwater oysters and the pearls they contained. That epic loss I have mentioned, in passing, in a story called 'A Journey to the Seven Streams', which you may find lying around somewhere.

How the running bitch was lost, and what Tommy Mullan said when he heard the news, was told to me by a friend called George McCanny when I was tied down (1938–9), in that orthopaedic hospital.

Here, also and as we all know, is the Clogher valley of South Tyrone, the country of William Carleton and of the *Traits and Stories of the Irish Peasantry*. Here in the late 1940s, as I've said, I had a happy time cycling hither and yon, and talking to Wilson Guy, and to Annie McKenna who then lived in Carleton's father's cottage, now a museum, and thinking I should write something in honour of William Carleton, and camping with my old schoolfriend, Frank Fox, then teaching school here in the town of Ballygawley: and drinking, me not Frank, in Con Corrigan's pub in the town of Clogher.

Research, by God! Drin to the bird of time!

Well, Mr Flood, if you insist I might.

Here at the roundabout at Ballygawley the New Omagh Road, to which John Montague wrote a hymn, begins. Here I give a moment's memory to the good days Frank Fox and Larry Loughran, and myself and many others, had, struggling with our native language at Rannafast on the rocks of the Rosses in West Donegal.

From this roundabout the road to the left goes to Belfast, and Belfast is another story.

On to Dublin then, through Monaghan town from which town came that beautiful damsel of fame and renown, a gentleman's daughter called Flora who, in the mighty ballad, stood up in her coach for to watch the parade of the Inniskilling Dragoons.

And in which town, I mean Monaghan, that much-referred-to brother was born, here in Glasslough Street and under the shadow of the great cathedral spire.

FOURTEEN

Evensong

In twelve hours I get from London to San Francisco, a city I have not visited in twenty-one years, and express myself gratified to find that it is still there, and am well welcomed by Liadhain O'Donovan Cook, daughter of Frank O'Connor and by my dear friend, Michael McCone. On a Monday night I get there. They give me a few hours to draw my breath and stretch my legs and then tell me, because they have to, that the brother has died in his sleep on the Sunday night, about the time I was over Iceland, or somewhere, and a long way from Bundoran where he died, and from the plantation and haunted graveyard of Clanabogan where he had once rested and sheltered from the rain in the company of the undisturbing dead: 'Real nice quiet people in Clanabogan. Not one of them said a word to me.'

He spoke to me clearly enough over that long distance.

Then one of my privileges during my stay in that amazing city was to be allowed to speak for fifteen minutes at Evensong in the vast Grace, Episcopalian, Cathedral.

From far away, farther even than Bundoran or Ballyshannon, the brother may have dictated me the text: and, fair being fair, I talked about him. He would have been amused, for my pulpit performances have not been numerous. His amusement, and his influence and good wishes, almost certainly averted the thunderbolt which, otherwise, might have wiped out his baby-brother, and the cathedral, and the congregation: all innocent people.

177

Even the Master of Thunderbolts may be off target and, I have heard it said, sometimes injures the innocent when He is trying to get at the guilty.

God, it may seem, never got good marks in gunnery.

But here is the text my brother may have sent me and here is my comment thereon:

From Revelations I read:

> Then he showed me the river of the water of life, bright as crystal,
> flowing from the throne of God and of the Lamb through the middle
> of the street of the city; also on either side of the river, the tree of life
> with its twelve kinds of fruit, yielding its fruit each month; and the
> leaves of the tree were for the healing of nations.

What I see as I read that, are rivers I have, you might say, intimately known in my own country and, also, great rivers I have seen, in passing, in other lands: and this evening I think of a man who loved rivers and the trees that grew beside them and who, also, all his life wished to visit San Francisco and to feast on the view, by day or by night, from Telegraph Hill.

How I know about all that it is easy to explain. He was the first man I ever heard make mention of San Francisco. He was giving me to read, when I was about three feet high, an adventure story called, as far as I remember, 'South Sea Gold'. The name of the author I cannot recall. It was a simple tale and uncomplicated reading for a young fellow and, right at the beginning, there was something or other about Telegraph Hill. The description whetted in me, also, a desire to see the place and I have done so. The man I mention, through this or that accident, never did.

There were many other things about him. To begin with he was a fisherman: a rod-and-line man on lake or riverbank and a genuine disciple of Izaak Walton in that he could quote the man, ad lib. And in all the business of life and in his relations with his fellowmen he displayed the quiet and patience, and consideration of small details, that the complete angler should possess. His favourite rivers were the Strule, the Camowen and the Drumragh in the County of Tyrone in the North of Ireland: they are part of the riverine system that issues to the sea, by Derry City, as the River foyle and Lough Foyle: 'Where

Foyle, her spreading water, rolls stately to the main There, Queen of Erin's daughters, fair Derry pitched her reign.'

Or so the song says.

Later in life he had a great fancy for the Glencar river, that Glencar that we will all know about from the poetry of William Butler Yeats.

His favourite lakes were the majestic Lower Lough Erne that goes to the sea by Belleek and Ballyshannon, in County Donegal, and here I think I have stumbled on part of his meaning, a small lake called Loch an Bhradáin, or the Lake of the Salmon, hidden in a secret corner of high moorland on the borders of Counties Tyrone and Fermanagh. For it may have been that his interest was not so much in catching fish as in going out into God's quiet places, and bringing friends with him to high moorlands and the banks of mountain streams where the moorcocks crow, and the linnet sings his sweet notes so pleasing.

His business in life took him, and kept him there most of his time, in parts of Ireland that he dearly loved: the northwestern counties of Donegal, Sligo, Leitrim, Mayo and inward to Cavan, Monaghan, Roscommon and Longford. That attachment of his to the solitudes and the mountain streams meant that he instinctively preferred the wilder places. He was a commercial man and dealt straight on with individual stores and storekeepers, so that his route often took him away from towns and by pleasant and intimate byroads. And everywhere he went his name for fair dealing went before him and remained behind him, and will for a long time. He was no fool – he was, indeed, as tough as they come – but he was a just man and to be known to be in any way associated with him meant that something of his good reputation rubbed off on you. He was brusquely but practically helpful to the weaker and underprivileged among our scattered and wandering brotherhood.

In his earlier years he was somewhat involved in Irish revolutionary, or underground, politics in relation to the partition of Ireland and the problems of the Six Counties of the northeast: and as a continuation of what he would have regarded as a brave and honourable tradition. But the unfortunate and often appalling events of the last nineteen years reduced him, I have heard, to the business of giving to the young what reasonable and restraining advice he could. He knew Earl Mountbatten and the murder of that aged man, who had so loved and trusted Ireland, afflicted him with a sad silence into which one did not dare to intrude.

But I heard him speak with sour humour of the odd fellows who had cut on the face of Ben Bulben mountain, and so as to be visible and legible for miles, the message: 'Brits Out.' And desecrated an ancient mountain with a message of hatred. That mountain already had its tragic legends and memories.

Did they mean so that Mountbatten could read it from his home at Classiebawn by the Sligo sea?

For the man I speak of had walked too long by the river of crystal of the water of life, to feel anything but utter sadness at what man could do to man: he had walked under those trees whose leaves were for the healing of nations.

He was my elder, or rather eldest, brother. The brother who came after him, and before me, died young. The man I am speaking of died quietly in his sleep on last Sunday night when I was somewhere in the air. A friend of mine in Dublin tried to contact me by 'phone in Heathrow Airport but by that time I had left the coast of Scotland and may have been somewhere over Iceland. There was no way in which I could have stood by his graveside in Ballyshannon, high over the river Erne. Yet I know he would have preferred me to be here to fulfil my undertakings in the city he had so often wished to visit, to mention his name in this great cathedral, and to walk and remember him on Telegraph Hill.

For many years he had lived between Bundoran and Ballyshannon and if, from the back of his house he crossed a few fields, he could look down on the Erne finally surrendering itself to the ocean by way of Donegal Bay. The poet William Allingham had written the great song about that river and that confluence. I quote four lines:

From Dooran to the Fairy Bridge and round by Tullan Strand,
Level and long, and white with waves, where gull and curlew stand:
Head out to sea when on your lee the breakers you discern! –
Adieu to all the billowy coast, and winding banks of Erne.

Lines three and four I would like to see on his gravestone.
So with a prayer, or something similar, I end this book.
And San Francisco is a mighty fine crossroads.